Derrida and Africa

African Philosophy
Critical Perspectives and Global Dialogue

Series Editors: Uchenna B. Okeja, Rhodes University; and Bruce B. Janz, University of Central Florida

Editorial Board: Anthony Appiah, Valentine Mudimbe, Gail Presbey, Achille Mbembe, Robert Bernasconi, Samuel Imbo, Tsenay Serequeberhan, Thaddeus Metz, Katrin Flikschuh, Niels Weidtmann, Christine Wanjiru Gichure, Kai Kresse, Joseph Agbakoba, Souleymane Bachir Diagne, Dismas. A. Masolo, Pedro Tabensky

The *African Philosophy: Critical Perspectives and Global Dialogue* book series aims to promote emerging critical perspectives in different branches of African philosophy. It serves as an avenue for philosophers within and between many African cultures to present new arguments, ask new questions, and begin new dialogues within both specialized communities and with the general public. By merging the critical and global dimensions of thoughts pertaining to important topics in African philosophy, this series beams the lights and rigour of philosophical analysis on topical as well as classical questions reflective of the African and African diaspora search for meaning in existence. Focused on the best of African philosophy, the series will introduce new concepts and new approaches in philosophy both to intellectual communities across Africa, as well as the rest of the world.

Titles in the series:

Afro-Communitarian Democracy, by Bernard Matolino
A Discourse on African Philosophy: A New Perspective on Ubuntu and Transitional Justice in South Africa, by Christian B. N. Gade
The Rule of Law and Governance in Indigenous Yoruba Society: An Essay in African Philosophy of Law, by John Ayotunde Isola Bewaji
Disentangling Consciencism*: Essays on Kwame Nkrumah's Philosophy,* Edited by Martin Odei Ajei

Derrida and Africa

Jacques Derrida as a Figure for African Thought

Edited by Grant Farred
Afterword by Jean-Paul Martinon

LEXINGTON BOOKS
Lanham • Boulder • New York • London

Published by Lexington Books
An imprint of The Rowman & Littlefield Publishing Group, Inc.
4501 Forbes Boulevard, Suite 200, Lanham, Maryland 20706
www.rowman.com

6 Tinworth Street, London SE11 5AL

Copyright © 2020 by The Rowman & Littlefield Publishing Group, Inc.

All rights reserved. No part of this book may be reproduced in any form or by any electronic or mechanical means, including information storage and retrieval systems, without written permission from the publisher, except by a reviewer who may quote passages in a review.

British Library Cataloguing in Publication Information Available

Library of Congress Cataloging-in-Publication Data

The hardback edition of this book was previously catalogued by the Library of Congress as follows:

Library of Congress Control Number: 2019951228

ISBN: 978-1-4985-8189-9 (cloth)
ISBN: 978-1-4985-8191-2 (pbk.)
ISBN: 978-1-4985-8190-5 (electronic)

This volume is dedicated to:
Gerard Aching and Salah Hassan.
Thank you for supporting the project.

Contents

Acknowledgments ix

Introduction: Africa, Still Remains xi
    Grant Farred

1. The Place That Is Not Here: Derrida's Africa and the Haunting of Place 1
    Bruce B. Janz

2. Deconstruction as Diaspora: On Derrida, Africa, and Identity's Deferral 17
    John E. Drabinski

3. Jacques Derrida: Figure of Maternal Thought 33
    Nicolette Bragg

4. Setting, an Example: Derrida's South Africa (and Ours) 47
    Jan Steyn

5. Jacques Derrida as an African Philosopher: Some Considerations from Francophone African Philosophy 65
    Kasereka Kavwahirehi

Afterword: Respect for Derrida and Africa 85
    Jean-Paul Martinon

Index 95

About the Editor 99

About the Contributors 101

Acknowledgments

I would like to acknowledge the support of the Institute for Comparative Modernities and Africana Studies & Research Center (Cornell University) in making this project possible.

To Ms. Renee Milligan for her administrative assistance and to Ms. Jana Hodges-Kluck for her editorial nous and the sense of calm she brought to the project.

Introduction

Africa, Still Remains

Grant Farred

How are we to find a form for writing Jacques Derrida as a figure for African thought? After all, are we (not) in advance duty bound to follow in the spirit of Derrida's parenthetical determination procure a singular form, as Derrida does in his meditation—his mourning—on the work of Roland Barthes? To wit: "(This is the form that I was looking for, something that *suits* him, that concerns only him.)"[1] To find a "form" fitted to the work of thinking Derrida in/and Africa, Derrida in relation to Africa, Derrida as a thinker of Africa, as African—or, at the very least, Maghrebian—thinker, is a project that serves only to magnify the difficulty of procuring such a "form." What kind of thinking will it require precisely to secure that "form" which can accommodate Derrida to the location, relocation, dis-location that is at the heart of the series of questions, uncertainties, to, indeed, the very skepticism that proposing—and thinking— that constitutes the ground of *Derrida and Africa*. A ground, it must be said, that must itself be claimed before it can, as it were, be worked; and claimed, no less, at once, by turns, with confidence and diffidence, first through one mode and then the other; worked, as such, with determination and trepidation. Or, as Martin Heidegger urges us in relation to the "being of Da-sein," we do so with "care:"[2] we must think this ground that is Jacques Derrida "and" (which is also to think Derrida "in" Africa, as being "of" Africa) in its widest possible range of articulations. It is to think Derrida "and" in its many gradations, in its obviousness and in its more discreet, disguised and subtle permutations. That is to say, it is work that must be done with "care"—to think "and/in/of" (Africa) "carefully." This is, needless to say, a relation that cannot be disarticulated from alienation, a relation that brings into view questions of diaspora (Jewish and post-/colonial) as well as questions about the (Francophone) postcolonial and the condition of life in the metropole for the diasporized. These conditions include the political developments that specifically address the condition of the Algerian-born philosopher as much as it reveals the issues that arose in the remaking of post-War Europe in general. What we confront, squarely, then (and it should certainly come as no surprise), is Jacques Derrida, philosopher of the postcolonial who was already a postcolonial thinker before the term gained either currency (its use appears rampant; its institutional presence ubiquitous) or its current (which is to say, post-1960s) conceptual denotations.

This is the ground that Derrida establishes, has created and bequeathed to contemporary thinkers, precisely because of the many resonances that emanate from his relationship to his native Algeria. Out of what is designated here as an "in/and relationship to" that is the relationship, before itself already in question, a question, which *Derrida and Africa* seeks to address. It is a ground that this collection returns to, again. And, then, for good measure, again. It is this ground, and the intellectual orbit, which lies beyond, adjacent and even somewhat removed from the oeuvre, the figure, the haunting philosophical absence-presence that we designate "Jacques Derrida," that these chapters seek to cover.

Derrida and Africa does so in order to establish itself as the terms for positing Derrida as a thinker who, rooted or unrooted, uprooted or re-rooted/rerouted, as he might be, speaks, in one way or another, first in this register and then the other, to this place from which he was displaced. This place that, we might speculate, he was never able to, try as he might, re-place, place himself outside of, whether he was in Paris or Prague, New York or southern California. Derrida, as has been argued elsewhere,[3] haunted by this place—the El Biar of his childhood and youth—that he returned so poignantly and provocatively in his work. In his contribution to this collection, Bruce Janz attends, with a deft interrogative touch, to precisely this question—Derrida and place. To propose Janz's argument as an interrogative, what is this "place that is not here?" John Drabinski too, is preoccupied with this question, and Drabinski's is addressed directly to thinker and place. "What," asks Drabinski, "is Africa to Derrida?" This is a line of inquiry that, Drabinski recognizes, already has its corollary—its companion question, if you will—contained within it. Contained within it, that is, as inversion: "What is Derrida to Africa?"

As such, the Derridean text that should cast the longest shadow over this project, should, rightly speaking, be *Monolingualism of the Other Or The Prosthesis of Origin*. (*Le Monolinguisme de l'autres: Ou la prosthese d'origine*).[4] *Le Monolinguisme de l'autres*, a Derridean work that must be apprehended as, first and above, a series of interrogatives, affirmations, refutations, disputations about growing up in El Biar. It is also a reflection on what it was like to be a Jewish schoolboy during World War II in Algiers and it is clearly a deeply painful moment of coming face-to-face with the facticity of French anti-Semitism. Last, but certainly not least, *Le Monolinguisme de l'autres* takes up the question of what it means to grapple with the condition of being a "Franco-Maghrebian." All in all, one might remark, *Le Monolinguisme de l'autres* must be understood as Derrida conducting a very public argument with himself. In the process, of course, he—whether he chooses to do so or not—invites us into the difficulty of accounting for himself as a diasporic, anti- and postcolonial thinker; lines of investigation that limn, as much as they inform, the Janz and Drabinski chapters especially.

No wonder, then, that the question of "form" assumes such urgency. After all, is there a "form" possible that will account for the taking up of (all) these issues? Derrida in/and Africa, how and where does one begin to think such a "form?" If nothing else, of this we can be sure. Such a "form" must be crafted, such a "form" that can think Derrida in/and/of, in relation to Africa and that can think Derrida as (being) of Africa. It remains to be, *l'avenir*, to be made, this "form," assuming such an autochthonous shape as Derrida's oeuvre affords it. It demands "care," this indeterminable "form."

It must also, however, be made by thinking Derrida in/and/of Africa; it must take its contours from his oeuvre but there must also be license to invent, to "shape" Derrida, as and when the need arises. (It is safe to assume that it arises, this need. The chapters in the volume testify to this need.) However, to find a "form" that fits Derrida in his relation to Africa, to find a "form" that may very well be, at first and for a long time afterward (perhaps forever), ill-fitting. A "form," that raises questions about itself as the "form" made to fit Derrida, the thinker of Africa. To find and then stay with such a "form" because the supposition is, as it must be, that only an ill-fitting, a poorly fitted "form," a philosophical garment made from tawdry stuff, such is the quality of "material" that is to hand, from what Derrida has handed us, can do the work of thinking *Derrida and Africa*. All this so that we might, as Michel Foucault says of his determination to critique neo-liberalism in its specificity (and not as though it were indistinguishable from everything else), "try to grasp it in its singularity."[5] To try to "grasp" Derrida in his "singularity," in his "singularity" as a thinker of and for Africa. To think, metonymically, the place of hilltop El Biar in relation to Algiers and to think Derrida in/and Algeria. It is, furthermore, to explore—as Kasareka Kavwahirehi does in his contribution to the collection—what it means to locate Derrida in/and continental and global Africa. What kind of African thinker, to follow Kavwahirehi in his pursuit (in the spirit of Janz and Drabinski), is Derrida? Presuming that he is, of course, an African thinker at all. A matter that this collection, in one way or another, considers as a necessarily unsettled—ir-resolvable—issue, which is precisely why it demands (repeated) address. Why and how Derrida matters to and in contemporary Africa is the issue that Jan Steyn's chapter takes up, and, indeed, makes a case for an almost poetic register.

Of necessity, then, *Derrida and Africa* undertakes this thinking of Derrida fully cognizant that it be marked by both a genealogical breadth and constitutive lacks. (Genealogical, that is, in Foucault's sense of it being a discontinuous but evocative project; the chapters all, in terms of one question or another, recall each other, but there is no single thread that runs through them; or, for that matter, ties them together.) After all, the collection neither addresses Derrida as philosopher (a terrain which is, of course, well covered) nor as "simply" (or only, or exclusively) "African." More than anything, then, *Derrida and Africa* marks a point of negative intersection. It is a writing where the two insufficiencies of record meet: it is a place of articulation; it is a placeholder, a necessarily temporary writing, which seeks to hold (down) a place—a starting point—for what might be. Is it possible to name Derrida in/and relation when no relation, no "ground," as such, exists? What kind of violence is that? What kind of thinking might emerge from this violence? Are there any other conditions under which such a thinking might emerge, with or without violence? Axiomatically, then, *Derrida and Africa* draws on, invokes, references and engages Derrida as philosopher but only rarely with the kind of depth that marks most scholarship of this Derridean variety. Similarly, this volume locates Derrida's thinking within Africa as such; and, again, it only once—without too much depth or duration—seeks to place Derrida within the broader project that is African philosophy.

In short, *Derrida and Africa* is a collection that takes full advantage, without always being able to account for the risks such a venture entails, of the "ground" it has created for and by itself. As such, it is no more than a speculative gesture. A thinking of in/and that grasps toward Derrida as a philosopher who is engaged with or might himself be grappling with "Africa" (or Algeria, or . . .), Derrida as a thinker whose philosophy is open to being taken up by another kind of iteration, whose philosophy is addressing questions other than what is at first apparent. Differently phrased, it draws what appears to be axiomatic into question so to make the axiom the point of first questioning.

The speculative, then, as that which is not reckless but responsible to Derrida in such a way as he might not himself have been able to construct (the concomitant, necessary) a philosophical responsibility. The introductory question about "form" and the attempt to produce a "ground" for the thinking that is *Derrida and Africa* must then be understood as the most preliminary—but by no means insignificant—steps toward establishing a responsible speculation. A speculation a priori dissatisfied with its constitutive insufficiencies but also willing to work within the terms— such as they are—that these very insufficiencies make possible. A collection, then, always in struggle with itself, with Derrida, but, throughout, it works diligently to be felicitous to what it does not, and cannot, with any authority, "know," as it were. What remains, however, is that *Derrida and Africa* works, works (burrows) away at, works with, Derrida in trying to understand what might be contained in what clearly functions—in spirit and in deed, if not in word—as a titular conjuncture: "in/and/of." A project, then, conceived in relation to the '/' that itself marks, in advance of itself, an un-/iterable conjuncture. A project that must be, it can do no other, tentative and unsure of itself from the very beginning. Tentative, speculative, and yet resolutely convinced of the responsibilities imposed by the responsibilities that attach themselves to the '/'.

TO PROCEED FROM MOURNING

To understand Derrida, then, in the terms of, as he says of Roland Barthes in *The Work of Mourning*, demanding a "certain composition,"[6] a "certain" skill and facility in the art of "composing" the life of the friend who is being mourned. Barthes is among the friends whose intellectual legacies, from which Derrida himself has, of course, inherited, are reflected upon in the *Work of Mourning*. There are others too, among them Michel Foucault, Gilles Deleuze and Louis Althusser (to whom the most poignant dedication is offered). In the essay "The Deaths of Roland Barthes," which turns on Barthes' first (*Writing Degree Zero*) and last (*Camera Lucida*) works, Derrida suggests that Barthes' writing be approached as "music." (Although Derrida's focus is on Barthes' first and last writings, he also spends a fair amount of time on *S/Z*, which is arguably Barthes' most famous work.) Barthes' work constitutes, to extend—and, distend, and disturb, too—the metaphor, a kind of poetry. As such, Derrida offers Barthes' work in terms of the truth of poetry it seeks to bring into being. That is, in all his work Barthes is arching and aching toward a felicitous writing, a writing that can bear his truth,[7] a "formal" difficulty that Fredric Jameson names the search for a "style"[8] in his study of Jean-Paul Sartre.

In the process of, as it were, putting mourning to music (making poetry of it), Derrida acknowledges that he cannot but commit a certain kind of violence against the friend whom he mourns. "I disfigure, I wound," Derrida admits (Derrida, *Mourning*, 44). However, under no circumstances must Derrida's admission be mistaken for an apologia. It does not trouble him that he is either "disfiguring" or "wounding" Roland Barthes. In order to mourn Barthes, in order to grapple with how Barthes did his work, Derrida must do violence—injustice, as such—to Barthes. Derrida can only come to terms with how Barthes' work affected him and continues to influence him, through/by doing violence to his subject. Derrida can only pay tribute to how Barthes locates his love for his mother (that figure, the mother—if not quite Barthes' mother—upon which Nici Bragg's chapter in this volume turns) in the photograph, Derrida can only properly name and apprehend Barthes' critique of photography, through doing violence to this figure whom he mourns. A figure, of course, whom he admires greatly. As Derrida reminds us of our political responsibility toward—for—justice, "One must never keep silent about the imprecation of the just."[9] (Of course, the mother is that figure who must be apprehended in any articulation of Derrida in/and Africa, so iconographic and dominant a symbol is the mother in the philosophy and vernacular of Africa's—political imagination. "Mother Africa," Africa as the "Mother" of human civilization, mean that Derrida in/and Africa must pass through the frame, through the experience that is the Mother. An experience in which birth, death and mourning feature prominently, these self-same features of which Bragg's chapter, in and on its distinct terms, reminds us.) In doing violence to the figure who is being mourned Derrida reminds us about something important. The only way which to do justice to thinkers such as Barthes, Foucault, Emmanuel Levinas and so on, is to treat them in their "singularity:" to think the figure in/on his own terms, to discern the poetry or the "music" that the thinker has composed.

The logic of "disfigurement," then, must be understood as, firstly, recognizing the rationale for the "wound" (what mode of thinking is it that the "wound" provokes? Mourning, melancholia, the desire for a new morning and the very prospect of death, notwithstanding, of course), and then addressing—not "dressing" or "salving"—the "wound." That is, acknowledging and working toward the proper name of the "wound." More than that, however, it is to identify the name as that name that is the only name worth—worthy of—"disfiguring."

To write "disfigurement" as no less than the Barthian project. On this question, Barthes is poetic: "nothing is more unfaithful than a colorless writing; mechanical habits are developed in the very place where freedom existed, a network of set form hem in more and more the pristine freshness of discourse."[10] To disfigure so is to restore the "pristine freshness of discourse," to do away with the restrictive forces that "hem in more and more" the innovative potentialities of "discourse" and, from the very beginning, to resist the infidelity that is "colorless writing." No poetry that aspires to the lyricism or rhythm or joy of music can ever submit to the demands of "colorless writing," of writing that is, shall we say, devoid of *jouissance* (pleasure, interrupted or no).

POETIC FORM

What a thing it is to undertake the work of writing—"colorfully," dare one suggest?—Jacques Derrida in/and/of Africa. Furthermore, to know that such a project can only be achieved through a rigorously poetic stipulation: the creation of a "form" that strives for, that inclines, determinedly, toward, the kind of music Derrida finds in Barthes. This is also, we are now sure, a distinct "form." After all, we now know how committed Barthes was to writing against precisely those "mechanical habits" that rob us of our ability to write/writing with the "freedom"—of expression, of experimentation, of philosophical contemplation—that once "existed." This "freedom" is vital to nothing less than our ability to think, a thinking that might very well proceed (the risk is unavoidable, one knows before one even begins), as Barthes says (writing about photographs of his mother), "by an infinite series of adjectives."[11] It would be massively unsatisfactory to write through "an infinite series of adjectives," because that would reduce writing to, much like the banality of electoral politics, the adjectival—a "series" of superlatives entirely devoid of meaning or content. As a matter of sentence construction ("writing" in its grammatical sense), it would avoid the difficulty that is thinking, that is precise phrasing. Such a writing can only be arrived at through nouns and verbs, part of speech that are less obfuscating and entirely more functional—verbs and nouns are altogether more elementary (alimentary) parts of speech. After the "adjectives," the few or the many of them, it matters not, have been stripped away, only the fundamental parts of speech remain. What remains are those parts that have to be worked with, those parts with a tougher core, those parts that do not permit of adornment. The crucible of the sentence, its irreducible truth, can be contained in and carried only by verbs and nouns. The crucible parts of speech, those crucible parts that bring us as close to truth as possible, as Arthur Miller teaches us in his drama of that same title.

What remains in the crucible, as crucible, is a life-long confrontation with difficulty, a difficulty that begins with the self as, again, Miller's play makes tragically clear. (And, insofar as the elemental purity of what remains in the crucible after passing through the fire that is distillation, reducing everything to its core, fundamental elements, to its essence. We are, then, whether we like it or not, confronted with that vast array of claims that pertain to what is essential. And, once the specter of "essential" is raised, we are compelled to acknowledge the politics of essentialism. A rampant politics, one that requires a full-throated critique, post haste. Alas, that is a discussion which will have to be—with an unsparing diligence—taken up elsewhere. For our purposes, we will return to the question of "essence"—the indestructible elements of any object, of any material, of, any being?—in our discussion of Derrida's *Cinders*. Suffice it to say, for now, that the crucible, through the experience of the crucible, what is left is what remains. And what remains is what will, despite all manner of violence and destructive intent, indestructible, evidence not only of a certain resilience, but the first and final elements of an indictment of those forces that intend to destroy with the hope of leaving no evidence, no trace, as it were, of either their deed or their intent.) This is a difficulty Derrida knows well, a difficulty that he has nowhere grappled with so poetically—so gnomically, enigmatically—as in *Monolingualism, Or the Prosthesis of Origin*. Elsewhere, I have named this Derridean struggle "nostalgeria,"[12] a neologism overburdened by the evocation of condition—nostalgia—and nation—Algeria; or, nostalgia for the nation that was never his, that which he could never renounce, or, for that matter, fully embrace. "Nostalgeria" is a condition that cannot quite be reduced to "nostalgia for Algeria," but that resonance is, for both good and ill, endemic to the naming.

In some ways, Derrida's in/and relationship functions on the order of Jean-Luc Nancy's attempt to understand freedom through "an-archy," which begins with the dis-avowal of "origin." The "origin," Nancy writes, "removed from every logic of origin, from every archeology—of a singular and thus in essence plural arising whose being *as being* is neither ground, nor element, nor reason, but truth, which could amount to saying, under the circumstances, freedom."[13] According to Nancy, we would be right to wonder about the "truth of origin," and, with equal perplexity (a condition shared, if not quite with perplexity, as such, by Bragg, Drabinski, Janz and Kavwahirehi), to ponder what kind of "freedom" obtains in "origin." In short, we are met with the question of how it is we are to think "origin," other than to resist "every logic, every archeology" that pertains to it. Does this mean, because they are diametrically opposed outcomes, that "truth" excludes or absorbs into itself the very "ground(s), element(s) and reason" of "origin?" As much as Nancy complicates and intensifies the philosophical and political stakes that inhere in "origin," what remains above all else is how vexing, frustrating but never enervating it is to "locate" a thinker or an "Idea" (in the Kantian sense)/*eidos* in relation to a historical moment or a geopolitical space. That is, "freedom," in the sense that one is liberated from the issue, is never a possibility except insofar as it must be addressed—thought, relentlessly.

The difficulty of Nancy's "freedom" bears, in its particular way, on Derrida's relation to El Biar, to Algiers, to Algeria, colonized, sovereign, rent by fundamentalism and the dictatorial (most recently in the form of President Abdelaziz Bouteflika and his *"décideurs"* who monopolize *"le pouvoir"*—"the power"). This Nancian "freedom" bears on Derrida's relationship to the Maghreb. All which positions Derrida as thinker of, if not quite "from" "Africa" (although he is, in strictly geopolitical terms, that too, as the various contributors in this collection give articulation to). The elemental truth, to invoke Derrida, Africa, "still remains." In much the same way, that is, as Derrida's musings on Jean-François Bonhomme's photographs/photography of "Athens," assures Derrida that the birthplace of philosophy is still accessible. If nothing else, the spirit of Socrates, Plato, Xenophon, the demos and the polis "still remains." Resolutely, *Athens, Still Remains*. Elemental, haunting, spectrally irrepressible. "Africa, Still Remains." Here, there, here, there, like the music Barthes conjures up, everywhere. Obdurate, unforgettable, forgotten. Africa, everywhere. "Africa, Still Remains."

Much like the French language that he so loves but can never be, in his disaffection, in his boundedness to it, his. The line, as we well know, is memorable: "'I have only one language; it is not mine'."[14] Imagining, casting himself as, being held—and by no means, except in moments, of course, against his will—within the thrall of this "one language;" and yet, he insists, "it is not mine." Derrida can never quite comprehend the lifelong power of this "language" that "is not mine" has over him; over him, over the Jews—like him, like his family—first enfranchised (by the "Crémieux decree of October 24, 1870") and then disenfranchised (by Marshall Pétain in "October 1940") and then again enfranchised after the end of the war.[15] Finally, Derrida is made to acknowledge the—violent, life-affirming—power this "one language" is "not his" has over him and the Algerian people in toto (and all others colonized by the French and their language), "We were hostages of the French, enduringly [*à demeure*]; something of it remains with me, no matter how much I travel."[16] The French language, which is not his, will not, cannot, be shaken off, unlike the dust accumulated on the shoes after a long journey. No wonder then that, as he says, "something," how much? All of it? Just some?, "of it remains with me." French, the language learned in the hilltop neighborhood of El Biar, just above Algiers. How could it not "remain" with him? Derrida's location within/and/against this language is at once a sign of his fidelity to this language that is "not his" and of his having come into this language under the vagaries of anti-Semitism and colonialism. Together, in its conflict-ridden, life-generating inhabitation of Derrida, the ways in which these conditions co-exist mark the peculiarities of what Derrida names his "disorder of identity."[17] Is this not the best possible mode of negotiating a relationship to "identity," anti-, postcolonial or otherwise?

French, the language of this place that was not his. Dare we speculate? "I have only one place; it is not mine." The chapters collected here do, indeed, more than speculate about Derrida's place within this language. They write Derrida as being of that place that is/is not his.

Africa, still . . .

Africa in its turbulent, undercurrent, mutinous, always resisting itself into language, this one or that, in its subterranean stillness. Africa, lying in wait, awakened by Derrida's interest in South Africa, his opposition to apartheid, his regard for Nelson Mandela and the anti-apartheid struggle. Derrida in South Africa today, in the midst of various mobilizations of philosophy and identity, is how Steyn locates Derrida in this collection.

"UNLOCATABLE"

Writing about the "*metonymic* operation" of Barthes' "*punctum*" and "*studium*," Derrida argues for their constitutive relation. The "uncoded *punctium*" "composes with the 'always coded' *stadium*" so that it, the former (P) "belongs to it [S] without belonging to it and is unlocatable within it;

it is never inscribed in the homogeneous objectivity of the framed space but instead inhabits or, rather, haunts it."[18] Belonging-without-belonging, relation-sans-relation (on the order of Édouard Glissant, a familiar figure in Drabinski's work[19]), bound to-it as an everyday act of resistance and attachment—held "hostage," gladly. In this way, much like P "inhabits or, rather, haunts" S (and surely the inverse is equally true; at the very least it is imminently possible), Derrida is "haunted" by El Biar. The hilltop neighborhood functions, in this regard, as the "metonymic operation" of Derrida the Algerian, Maghrebian, North African, African. All these names, geographical, geopolitical markers, political conditions, concatenated, in struggle, is what makes Derrida, then, now, now and then, "unlocatable within . . . the homogeneous objectivity of the framed space," however one understands or identifies these "spaces," this "space" or that one. "Unlocatable," sometimes in the terms offered by Janz and Kavwahirehi, as the mark of imprecision, not as the condition of interpellation. That is, under the condition of being consumed by this "space" rather than that other "space."

"Unlocatable" as the generative difficulty that is thinking Derrida, at any one moment, in his relation to, say, El Biar rather than the Maghreb, to think him as the disenfranchised Jew and not the Arab or the Berber. "Unlocatable" as the violence of relation, as the colonialist imperative to make place definitive, as the resistance to being named finally—the impossibility of a once and for all naming. "Unlocatable" as, following Nancy, the "freedom" to think the "truth" of the "homogeneous objectivity of the framed space." Again. To refuse the impulse that is "homogeneous objectivity." To think, at once, for and against the obstinacy that is homogeneity. That is, to simultaneously refuse to recognize Derrida as and to insist on representing him as Derrida the disenfranchised Sephardic Jew or Derrida as the modern intellectual inheritor of his Algerian forbearer, Augustine, Bishop of Hippo.

As such, we are free to write our mourning of Derrida, to mourn—and, in so doing, to celebrate, this celebration that is also the unrepentant political act of inscribing a claim: Derrida as African, as African made so through intellectual and political appropriation masquerading as a certain mode of propriety. To now write him as such, as if such a writing were even conceivable; that is, to throw his thinking, violently, into and against another light entirely. To state, establish, and make a case for the claim that he is of Africa and because of the irrefutable force of "origins," must, because of this, be thought again. A new condition, if not a dictum, although they may be indistinguishable forms insofar as they are borne out of the presumption that this is a "valid" or philosophically or politically sustainable and just, yes, just, claim. This condition that insists that thinking Derrida proceeds from the ground that "Africa" remains, like so many traces of the trace, illegible, scattered throughout the oeuvre that is Jacques Derrida's thinking. El Biar, Algiers, Algeria, the Maghreb, the event of disenfranchisement, the Shoah, Africa, its remains, like the remnants of the ashes, iterated in his work. Proceeding from an ill-defined notion of "origins," compelled into ill-fitting geopolitical attire, a flawed project and yet one that retains about it the patina of absolute necessity.

CINDERS AND ASHES

As with *Monolingualism*, Derrida's work in *Cinders*—the text that preoccupies Drabinski in this volume—takes its cue from a single sentence. A "phrase" that, as Derrida says, "came to me, as though in spite of me; to be more precise, it returned, unique, uniquely succinct, almost mute," "fifteen years ago."[20] This phrase, as Derrida recounts, has long since haunted him—for the "first time (was it the first time?) . . . at the end of a book, *Dissemination*."[21] The phrase in question is "'there are cinders there,' 'cinders there are' [*il y a là cendre*]."[22] The force of "return," despite his best efforts to lay it to rest, which is almost invariably linked to or articulated through the power of haunting, marks and mars—in that it gives us to thinking, especially to thinking violence, the law, the history of the law and violence—Derrida's oeuvre. All of which attests to those effects that will not abide silencing. It is true that the phrase, "*il y a là cendre*," seems as if it is barely audible, as if it has been reduced to a very low volume. However, this does not mean that it was in danger of not being heard. Its audibility, its volubility, if you prefer, owes much to the force of return. To, we might say, the resilience of the "cinder," its ability to leave its mark on Derrida's thinking and, then, to find its way back to the level of his consciousness. The historical disturbance contained in the trace is always more powerful than the desire or the inclination or the determination to put things, difficult issues, to rest. For "fifteen years" of Derrida's life, the "phrase" can be stilled, as it were. But it will never be silenced. Here again we should keep in mind Derrida's injunction about the political infelicity that is "silence" in the face of the "imprecation of the just."

Because of how Derrida opens himself up to haunting, because of his willingness to attend to the phrase that insists upon the right to return, no doubt at the most inopportune moment, when it is least wanted, when it is likely to cause the most discomfort (thus reestablishing its standing as a catalyst for thinking), what he makes possible is the return not only of the phrases he catches, as it were, but the other phrases, questions and conundrums that follow in the allusive wake of the "originary phrase." The phrase that instigates "return" never, of this we can be sure, travels alone. It always travels in the company of other "phrases," and is almost certainly accompanied by other difficulties, difficulties, we might say, that emanate from those elements that "remain," un-stilled, restless, persistent. The "phrase" is most likely probing, awkward, and eminently unwelcome. That is precisely why it has been kept at bay for "fifteen years." However, "fifteen years" is not forever, not by any stretch of the imagination, and the "phrase" will endure long beyond that. It will endure into the event.

It is for this reason that the "phrase" is foreboding. We remember Derrida's love for *Hamlet*, after all: "Something is rotten in the state of Denmark."[23] However, because it threatens—we might even say promises or, to go one step further, we can assert that it guarantees—or contains within its articulation and grammar, in its structure, in its form, the germ of the event or the event itself. "Something" is always "rotten" somewhere. This means, invariably, that the event is (potentially) detectable (discernible, legible) in any "phrase." And yet not, because the event is felicitous—picky, finicky, persnickety, we might even suggest, all the while reminding ourselves of Nancy's fealty to the event as nothing other than the "surprise" that emerges out of "freedom"[24] —to itself, it is precise in its language, in how it speaks or announces itself.

What the event, as such, demands, is our accountability to it, our accountability especially in the face of being "surprised" by the event. (The logic of the event is that it would appear to refuse logic. That is because of the temporal contradiction upon which the event is founded. The event is punctual only to itself. Consequently, we live in expectation of the event and have no idea as to when it will manifest itself. Therefore, despite our eagerness for it to arrive, despite our apparent preparedness and perhaps even our impatience—when will it come? Why has it not arrived yet?—the event always takes us by "surprise.") Derrida understands this relation to history, to accountability, to the "phrase." He understands it only too well. In a language redolent with Shakespearean overtones (bringing to mind, in rapid succession, *Hamlet* and Derrida's *Specters of Marx*, a text in which Shakespeare, as we well know, has a prominent discursive function), Derrida admits of his accountability to the "phrase." Derrida acknowledges his having to answer, like first Marcellus enjoins Horatio to do, as Hamlet's closest and most trusted friend and then the prince himself, to the "phrase."

In a language full of "ghostly demarcations," Derrida tells us about his experience of living with the ghost: "For nearly ten years, the specter's comings and goings, unforeseen visits of the ghost. The thing spoke all on its own. I had to explain myself to it, respond to it—or for it."[25] Derrida must speak. He must speak under the sign of indictment, speak for fear of losing himself. There is something which he must not only address, called on to "respond" as he is, but there is, potentially, something for which he—and he alone?, we are free to wonder—is being called to account. He must answer for "it," for that which he has done, or, not done, as the case might be.

In this way, in "accepting" his responsibility, in understanding himself as singularly accounting, in our reading, in our apprehension (we could easily say our "appropriation" or our instrumentalization or delimitation of him; "where" he must be thought from, etc.) of him, we are made heirs to his thinking. In engaging his thought, however, we confront the reality of our inheritance. The question, as such, bequeathed to us is not simply how we "respond" to Derrida. It is, in addition, to take up the difficulty of what it is that we must, in our turn, in our collaboration with him, make him and us "respond" to. More pertinently and pointedly, what is it that we must ask of Derrida and, ourselves, of course, that he does not, cannot, or has only insufficiently done, ask of himself. In other words, we have to put instrumentalization and the "inessentiality"—as Nancy would have it—of geopolitics to good philosophical use.

We are called upon, for our part, to speculate: to speculate responsibly by "responding" at once, by turns, one after the other, "to it" and for it." "To" what must we "respond?" To nothing other than thinking as such. "For" what we must think is an entirely more treacherous—speculative—endeavor. Of that we cannot be sure, ever, but it is the provocation and the demand that thinking Derrida, in his terms, against himself, in pursuit of our interests and investments, despite our better angels, because of our worst angels, that his work has left us, left us as his voluminous inheritance.

What is more, we cannot say that he did not warn us. In *Specters of Marx* he prepared us, gave us ample time to get ready: "the dead can often be more powerful than the living."[26] Of course, Derrida is himself writing here under a more ominous specter, that which Marx issues in the "Eighteenth Brumaire of Louis Bonaparte:" "The tradition of all the dead generations weights like nightmare on the brain of the living."[27] It is settled, then. The "power" of the dead is that they demand an address from the "living." It seems imperative not to allow Derrida's thinking to, over generations, assume a deadly "weight"—a fatal "weightiness," if you will. In order to avoid such an outcome, we must answer "for it." Answer for it precisely because we are so unsure as to what exactly "it is."

Here, in this volume, we are following but one thread, one of the many that could potentially be "traced." Some of what is being followed will reveal itself with clarity and precision. Others will remain determinedly inaccessible. Some of our tracings will surely "yield" more insights, and more quickly, than others. Some, no doubt, will unravel, probably all too quickly. *Derrida and Africa* begins to imagine what it means to think Derrida in his non-/relation to Africa. A relationship that is so hauntologically present—presented—through his dedication to the slain South African communist leader, Chris Hani, in *Specters*. This collection thinks him in the interrupted silence of his non-/relation to the Maghreb, which might be traced through the figure of St. Augustine, as in the "autobiographical" *Circumfession* or in the essay "Typewriter Ribbon," where Augustine, Rousseau and Paul de Mann are the central figures. These essays recognize the difficulty of his speaking El Biar, so poetically rendered in *Monolingualism*.

A FORM, A FIGURE, EVOKING, BORROWED FROM GREECE

In the spirit of William Carlos Williams, in the spirit of his magnificent "wheelbarrow" brevity, let us allow the following: So much depends upon Horatio's address, on him commanding the language to speak to the specter. To speak the specter, to speak spectrally. Another language, entirely; a language entirely familiar. So much depends upon Horatio speaking, nothing less than the fate of the state; the state that is now, courtesy of a regicide, an *etat voyou*. "Speaking to it," as we are well aware, resolves nothing. The tragedy, the collapse of the Danish royal house, is set in motion and with it the demise of the prince, his lover, his mother, stepfather...

But not without, but not before, as Hamlet's soliloquys (most notably "To be or not to be") bears ample testament, a serious wrestling with self, with what it means to be political in the world, with the immense (destructive) force of the political.

As he describes it, this is Derrida's struggle: "I would thus be able to settle up with it and then settle on leaving it, leaving it without leaving it without losing it. This was precisely my desire, or else the opposite: to distance myself from it without ever leaving it."[28] Here is Derrida's inability to "settle" the irresolvable matter of "leaving it without leaving it." Or, a prospect that seems worse, here Derrida articulates the threat of "losing it," a possibility that turns on the sentence "*Nous nous devons à la mort*" — "we owe ourselves to death." (Yet a further instance of Derrida subjecting a single sentence, a wonderfully knotted, entangled thought to extended philosophical contemplation.) Crudely cast, poorly translated, yet for all that evocative and familiar:

> *Nous devon nous-même à l'Afrique.*
> "We owe ourselves to Africa."
> "We owe our thinking to Africa."
> "We owe our thinking of Derrida to Africa."
> "Do we owe our thinking of Africa to Derrida?"
> "What does Derrida, what does Derrida's thinking, owe to Africa?"
> "How are we to think, to write, what we imagine Derrida 'owes' to Africa?"
> "Dare we cast it as a debt?"
> *Nous devon nous-même à l'Afrique.*
> *l'Afrique reste toujour.*

What a wrenching struggle. What a way to live, to learn to live. Then again, is there any other way to live? How does one live so that one under the condition of "leaving it without leaving it without losing it?" At least this much is clear: "it," we may figure it as a place or a state of mind and as such it cannot and will not be left either unspoken or unaddressed. (Let us be base, in Marx's sense, anyway, and name it alienation, intense psychological remove; the diaspora; or we can follow Derrida and name it the "ashes and sackcloth" of a life—that is, "cinders.") "It" will not be left behind, this "place," it refuses to be abandoned. This "place" is that place that will not be displaced or, by any means, replaced. This "place" is resolute in insisting on its (proper) place. All the while there remains, counterintuitively, the prospect of loss, the fear of "losing it." Of losing that which seems obstinate, unmovable, and beyond the logic of deracination. All the while, of course, it is that very specter, deracination, forced removal, upheaval, violent movement (the disenfranchisement of October 1940, the ongoing effects of the Crémieux of October 1870, little "October revolutions" pertaining only to the diasporized Jewish psyche, especially that psyche rooted in the Marrano experience), that makes immanent the perpetual threat of loss. Of place, of place in this or that society, of the right to determine the self—what Derrida also recognizes as "sovereignty."

Still, in the face of all this, alienation—or, at the very least, self-generated remove—is impossible. After all, in Athens, enthralled by death, Derrida pronounces that he sought to "set out from it without ever leaving it." What a debt, what a philosophical debt, death is owed. *l'Afrique reste toujour*. Africa remains. Africa remains. How it is that Africa remains must be thought. It will always remain: to be thought. Derrida's inability to "settle up with it and then settle on leaving it," the very definition of Derridean haunting, the very condition of living with the specter, of existing in its formidable shadow (the shadow that both protects and signals a zone of danger), returns Africa to us as the inexhaustible presence of "it." There is no escaping it. Africa can never be settled, not in Augustine's voluminous writings nor in the way in which it will never allow Derrida to leave it or to be, ever, released from it. There are many paths that can lead us to Derrida's thinking but every one of them will, finally, have to return to El Biar or some iteration of it . . . Algeria, the war of independence, the politics and history of the Maghreb . . . Africa, still remains, steadfast, unmovable as an "it" to be thought. Again. As if for the first time. As if we were just making Derrida's acquaintance, making our first acquaintance with his work.

Derrida remains to be thought. To be thought, again, on his terms, in our critique, as a figure of African thought.

So, when Derrida declares, "I have only one language; it is not mine," there is a specter to be addressed. (There is, as with the case of Roland Barthes—"The Deaths of Roland Barthes," with an accent on the plural, is how Derrida titles his "contemplation" in *The Work of Mourning*, more than one specter to be addressed, more than one haunting to be acknowledged.) But here the specter that looms largest, if not most ominously, is that specter which recognizes that Derrida can never, as it were, "settle" his accounts with Africa; and this means, of course, that he is never free to "leave it." He is never free to declare himself "free of it." In the rough, grating tones, albeit a tone always saturated by wistful regret, of Willie Nelson, "You are always on my mind." There is something indefatigable and relentless about the specter of Africa. It will not be shucked off, it will not be denied.

All of this means, of course, that we must, if only in the most perfunctory fashion, recognize the love that Derrida felt for, feels for, Africa. No matter that Africa, for too long in his work, and the commentary and the scholarship that derived from it, was made secondary—of lesser, or even no importance. Or, worse, in truth. Entirely ignored. Overwhelmed, as it were, by other facets, more recognizably "European" philosophical traditions or Western philosophical pursuits, Derrida's critique of phenomenology and logocentrism not least among the more obvious lines of inquiry that marked, marks, engagement with Derrida's work. In some measure, it is Derrida's doing. In other ways, it derives from the inability to understand what must always, for his whole life, has been "on his mind." "Always."

It is for these reasons that we are not free to free Derrida, to liberate him into that place which he can neither resolve ("settle") nor abandon ("leave"). The only freedom afforded (us) is to hold him to account, hold him to account in the very terms he articulates in writing on Athens, with the unlikely backdrop of a plaintive, self-indicting, Willie Nelson ballad. "This book," Derrida says of *Athens, Still Remains*, "bears the signature of someone keeping vigil and bearing more than one mourning, a witness who is doubly surviving, a lover tenderly taken by a city that has died more than once, in many times, a city busy watching over all that is noncontemporaneous within it . . ."[29] Derrida is the thinker who cannot "settle," who cannot "settle" on departure. He is the thinker who cannot ready himself to take leave of this city. He cannot do so in no small measure because it is love that binds him, his love of philosophy, of Socrates and the maritime intrigue that births philosophy, the hemlock cup, the *polis*, to this place. Derrida, for once and for all, bears more than a striking resemblance to that figure "burdened" with the "signature of someone keeping vigil and bearing more than one mourning." Perhaps we can now say that we knew what is "always" on Derrida's "mind."

It is "our time," our responsibility, one we both wrest to ourselves (claim, insist on, appropriate, share, all at once, all under the sign of hesitancy and assertion) in the name of "Derrida/El Biar/Algiers . . ." and a moment, a series of philosophico-political inclinations, commitments, if you insist, that we share with Derrida, in his name. (In this instance, it is entirely possible to argue, that there is very little, if anything, that separates "appropriation" from "sharing.") In the act of making his name,

"Jacques Derrida," speak, like Horatio, to the specter that lived in him, that was "always on his mind."

"OUT OF JOINT"

Derrida, we know, especially from his writing that runs from *The Work of Mourning* to *Without Alibi* to *Monolingualism*, and much more besides, is an expert on "keeping vigil." He knows how to watch over things, how to watch over his friends, especially those who have died. He knows how to keep their various spirits alive. All of which means, in a word, that Derrida knows both how to mourn and how to address the morning that comes in mourning's wake. He knows how to write the dead, how to write death, how to write it to and for the living. He knows, as it were, how to live "out of joint." That is why he enjoins us to think his "watching" carefully "over" his "noncontemporaneity" with El Biar, with Algeria, with Africa.

Long before Pétain's anti-Semitic act of October 1940, Derrida knew himself, before he knew himself, to be "out of joint" with Algiers. However, to be "out of joint" never constitutes a political release. There is no immunity from political responsibility, no inoculation against the effects of "out of jointness." This is the political lesson that Hamlet learned, tragically.

To live "noncontemporaneously" is to live a particular (some might prefer "privileged") relation to the moment from which the subject is alienated. "Out of jointness" demands its own accounting. The time, time itself, is ruthless and unyielding in this regard. It will "settle" for nothing less than a full explication of why it is that it (time) is not contemporary with itself; or, as Heidegger might insist, that is why we must not settle for the "vulgar concept of time."[30] Furthermore, from at least G.W. Liebniz on (how else are we to understand the time of the fold?), philosophy has accepted responsibility for explaining time's "out of jointness" with itself. Always, of course, with Shakespeare there to lend a helping hand.

It is for this reason that Derrida's "desire" is more than the source of (love and) conflict, although it is, at its most reductive level precisely that. Rather, Derrida's "desire" stands as—at once—an embracing of the dialectic ("This was precisely my desire, or else the opposite") and a submission to thinking in the terms of a time "out of joint" with itself. It is, in a word, to understand the impossibility of removing the self without—or, worse, if you insist—petitioning for the right to be, not to put too fine a point on it, disenfranchised. It is for this reason that the condition of being "out of joint," from Hamlet to Derrida, is always riddled—in the best possible way—with the complication that is an apologia, that apologia struggling to express itself as the desire for something else, the historic desire, as it were, that the time not "out of joint." The desire for, in short, the impossibility that is absolute contemporaneity.

All of which bears on and leads us to the crucial recognition that to learn to live noncontemporaneously is nothing less than learning to live. Learning to live, pure and simple, if we accept that learning to live is, of course, never a simple or a pure matter. It is never either a simple or a settled matter because learning to live is, necessarily, constitutively, tinged with and informed by regret, disappointment, self-reflection, loss, love and the prospect of what is not. The time is never "in joint." Time is never unto itself, exclusively; time is, in this sense, marked by the preponderance of what Heidegger understands as "vulgar." Time and being have to be thought, together, discretely, discretely in order to be "lived" together. Something almost entirely different from what Heidegger proposes in *Zeit und Sein*.

To learn to live noncontemporaneously is to know, to accept, what it means to live politically. It is to learn to live always under the sign of mourning. It is to learn to live always in expectation of and in preparation for mourning. It is to learn to live while undertaking the impossible task of repressing, of reducing to political silence, that place, that moment, when the hard truth presents itself, when it irrupts into life. All living must confront the effect of living noncontemporaneously. All living is "out of joint." All time, which also means every place, is in struggle with itself. All that differs is how and when that struggle manifests itself. All living, we are tempted to declare, is living . . . living for, in anticipation of, the event. Noncontemporaneity is, as such, the (first?) condition of the event.

NONCONTEMPORANEITY

"Out of joint" Africa—anti-Semitism, October 1870, October 1940, National Socialism, Pétain—made possible the conditions for Derrida's thinking. Precisely that Africa which Derrida had long been, had long continued to be, "out of joint" with, it is that Africa—that experience, in Nancy's sense—that "offered" itself, from the very beginning, as the instantiation par excellence of noncontemporaneity. The time, for philosophy but also for all of us, is always "out of joint." Every time is in struggle with itself. Every time is, and for this we are thankful, is in struggle, in bitter and often brutal, conflict with itself.

It is only noncontemporaneity which can give us philosophy. We know this from the moment that the ship returns from Delos to signal Socrates' death ("We owe ourselves to death."). It is only our noncontemporaneity that conditions necessary for the event can arise. It is only noncontemporaneity that can give us—give us over—to thinking.

We owe ourselves, our work, our thinking, our thinking of Derrida in this case, to noncontemporaneity. To thinking Derrida "out of place," "out of times"—let us afford ourselves the privilege of the plural—because any other mode of apprehension would do no justice what was "always on Derrida's mind:" Athens, El Biar, Paris, Algiers, Europe, Africa, the Maghreb, North America. Together, discretely. Discretely together. Neither one nor the other, no matter how one constructs the dyad (say, Algiers/Paris), "second best," neither one nor the other less loved. Both loved, both, to some immeasurable extent or the other, embraced, both, in their moments, capable of overwhelming, making of love—of loving them, Athens, El Biar, in their turn, bound by love, of place, of time, of their times, because of the places they are in (Derrida's) time—a life-long struggle. The battle with the self, that battle borne "out of joint," out of Derrida's (and our) "out of jointness." To find, to name, a time, a place, that is never free of the struggle to be free, free of the struggle for, in Nancy terms, freedom that can only emerge out of the condition of "out of jointness." That is the only way in which a Nancian "freedom" could be secured.

It is now possible to assert that all who "proclaim" on Derrida can only ever do so under the sign of the provisional. To "proclaim" Derrida is, then, always a precarious undertaking. Even, that is, if it does find that form of address, of writing, that, at the very least, wends its way, however circumspectly or insistently, through El Biar, Algiers, Algeria . . .

For this reason, our thinking of Derrida proceeds from a ground (a condition of thinking) that is at once, by turns, first that and then the other, provisional, assertive, hesitant, declarative, unsure of how to think a politics of relation, cautious, careless, about furnishing a series of relations for Derrida.

When we began by thinking Derrida in/and Africa, we could not have, surely we could not have, expected that our path would run along the tracks that it has. Through the many ruts and bumps that constitute the "Deaths of Roland Barthes" or the technical reflections on photography (and death) that Athens provokes. (Or, maybe Athens is no big surprise and Roland Barthes is only slightly more surprising. But surely not Willie Nelson.)

We have taken Derrida by surprise. We have taken ourselves by surprise.

However, if that is the case, then we have not attended closely enough to the oeuvre that is Jacques Derrida's work. We may agree or not on the paths that we have taken, on the byways that have seduced us, on the waystations in which we have sought shelter in (shelter from the gentle, persistent storm clouds that is Derrida's work). However, of this we have always been sure: we should never be surprised by where Jacques Derrida's work leads us. Especially, or, not, when we think Derrida from Africa, when we think Derrida in/and Africa, when we acknowledge the intensity of our claiming him, and the very dangers that such an appropriation risks.

We are, then, thinking Derrida in/and/of Africa under one of the most Derridean signs. Autoimmunity.

In making a claim, such a claim as the one we are making, such a claim to make, there is no other way to think Derrida in/and Africa than to imagine Derrida at once, and, of course, by turns, affirming such a claim, affirming our claim, and drawing it, again and again, into question.

Affirmation and interrogation. Affirmation and the need, no, the demand, for "justification" (which, of course, means that we are always, before ourselves, thinking for justice). This means that there is, to some extent or other, always an extant form for thinking Derrida, but that such a form, such a mode of inquiry and apprehension, can never escape our—and his, we suspect—founding suspicion: Africa, El Biar, Algiers, Algeria, the diasporized Sephardic Jew, displaced post-/colonial, was "always on Jacques Derrida's mind."

We know this, with provisional certainty, because he is never able to "settle it." What is more, neither are we. What is more, neither should we be.

To "settle it," the question of Derrida in/and Africa would amount to no less than circumscribing, undermining, circumventing, and doing no justice to what is on our minds as much as "it"—in the several iterations offered here, "it-"erations, that preoccupied Derrida. To learn to live is to do nothing less than embracing that particular difficulty that is most resistant to "resolution," and most disconcerting in its ability to "unsettle" us, and most stubbornly, day by day, decade after decade, remains "on our mind."

> Africa, Still Remains.
> *Nous devon nous-même à l'Afrique.*
> *l'Afrique reste toujour.*

What remains is still. It demands, amidst all the rancor that is our thinking Africa, a moment, as long as it takes, to be thought.

Africa remains, above all else, to be thought as, to what extent both should and should not concern us, as being of the thought of Jacques Derrida.

NOTES

1. Jacques Derrida, "Roland Barthes: November 12, 1915—March 26, 1980," *The Work of Mourning*, edited by Pascale-Anne Brault and Michael Naas, Chicago: The University of Chicago Press, 2001, 39 (original emphasis).

2. Martin Heidegger, *Being and Time*, translated by Joan Stambaugh, Albany: State University of New York, 1998, 378.

3. See Grant Farred, *The Burden of Over-representation: Race, Sport, and Philosophy*, Philadelphia: Temple University Press, 2018. This project is informed from beginning to end by Derrida, especially the final chapter, "I Think I Saw Jacques Derrida at the 2010 World Cup in South Africa."

4. Jacques Derrida, *Monolingualism of the Other Or The Prosthesis of Origin*, translated by Patrick Mensah, Stanford: Stanford University Press, 1998.

5. Michel Foucault, *The Birth of Biopolitics: Lectures at the Collége de France, 1978-1979*, translated by Graham Burchell, New York: Palgrave MacMillan, 2004, 130.

6. Jacques Derrida, *The Work of Mourning*, edited by Pascale-Anne Brault and Michael Naas, Chicago: The University of Chicago Press, 2001, 41.

7. In *The Birth of Biopolitics: Lectures at the Collège de France 1978-1979*, Michel Foucault conducts, in his critique of (the history of) neoliberalism, his own inquiry into what constitutes a regime of truth (*The Birth of Biopolitics: Lectures at the Collège de France 1978-1979*, translated by Graham Burchell, New York: Picador (Palgrave MacMillan), 2004.

8. Fredric Jameson, *Sartre: The Origins of a Style*, New York: Columbia University Press, 1984. In *Sartre*, Jameson argues that "style" as we now know it is a "modern phenomenon," one which is "somehow in itself intelligible, above and beyond the limited meaning of the book written in it, and beyond even those precise meanings which the individual sentences that make it up are designed to convey" (Jameson, *Sartre*, vii).

9. Jacques Derrida, *Specters of Marx: The State of the Debt, the Work of Mourning, & the New International*, translated by Peggy Kamuf, New York: Routledge, 1994, 42.

10. Roland Barthes, *Writing Degree Zero*, translated by Annette Lavers and Colin Smith (New York: Hill & Wang, 1983, 78.

11. Roland Barthes, *Camera Lucida: Reflections on Photography*, translated by Richard Howard, New York: Hill & Wang, 2010, 70.

12. Grant Farred, "Nostalgeria: Derrida, Before and After Fanon," *The South Atlantic Quarterly* 2013, Volume 112, Number 1.

13. Jean-Luc Nancy, *The Experience of Freedom*, translated by Bridget McDonald, Stanford, CA: Stanford University Press, 1993, 13.

14. Jacques Derrida, *Monolingualism of the Other Or The Prosthesis of Origin*, translated by Patrick Mensah, Stanford, CA: Stanford University Press, 1998, 1.

15. Derrida, *Monolingualism*, 17

16. Ibid

17. Ibid

18. Derrida, *Mourning*, 41

19. See, Drabinski, *Glissant and the Middle Passage: Philosophy, Beginning, Abyss*, Minneapolis: University of Minnesota Press, 2019.

20. Jacques Derrida, *Cinders*, translated by Ned Lukacher, Minneapolis: University of Minnesota Press, 2014, 3.

21. Ibid

22. Ibid

23. Shakespeare, *Hamlet*, Act I, Sc. 4. New York: Methuen, 1982.

24. In his critique of the "end of a relation . . . between being and history," Nancy argues for an "existent" in which "freedom surprises" itself, a condition in which the "existent is singularized, that is to say, exists according to the free and common space of its inessentiality" (Nancy, 16).

25. Derrida, *Cinders*, 4

26. Derrida, *Specters*, 48

27. Karl Marx, "The Eighteenth Brumaire of Louis Bonaparte," *Karl Marx: A Reader*, edited by Jon Elster, New York: Cambridge University Press, 1989, 277.

28. Jacques Derrida, *Athens, Still Remains: The Photographs of Jean-François Bonhomme*, translated by Pascale-Anne Brault and Michael Naas, New York: Fordham University Press, 2010, 7.

29. Derrida, *Athens*, 7

30. Heidegger, 385

WORKS CITED

Barthes, Roland, *Camera Lucida: Reflections on Photography*, translated by Richard Howard, New York: Hill & Wang, 2010.
———. *Writing Degree Zero*, translated by Annette Lavers and Colin Smith, New York: Hill & Wang, 1983.
Derrida, Jacques: *Athens, Still Remains: The Photographs of Jean-François Bonhomme*, translated by Pascale-Anne Brault and Michael Naas, New York: Fordham University Press, 2010.
———. *Cinders*, translated by Ned Lukacher, Minneapolis: University of Minnesota Press, 2014.
———. *Monolingualism of the Other Or The Prosthesis of Origin*, translated by Patrick Mensah, Stanford, CA: Stanford University Press, 1998.
———. *Specters of Marx: The State of the Debt, the Work of Mourning, & the New International*, translated by Peggy Kamuf, New York: Routledge.
———. *The Work of Mourning*, edited by Pascale-Anne Brault and Michael Naas, Chicago: The University of Chicago Press, 2001.
Drabinski, John, *Glissant and the Middle Passage: Philosophy, Beginning, Abyss*, Minneapolis: University of Minnesota Press, 2019.
Farred, Grant, "Nostalgeria: Derrida, Before and After Fanon," *The South Atlantic Quarterly* 2013, Volume 112, Number 1.
———. *The Burden of Over-representation: Race, Sport, and Philosophy*, Philadelphia: Temple University Press, 2018.
Foucault, Michel, *The Birth of Biopolitics: Lectures at the Collége de France, 1978-1979*, translated by Graham Burchell, New York: Palgrave MacMillan, 2004.
Heidegger, Martin, *Being and Time*, translated by Joan Stambaugh, Albany: State University of New York, 1998.
Jameson, Fredric, *Sartre: The Origins of a Style*, New York: Columbia University Press, 1984.
Marx, Karl, "The Eighteenth Brumaire of Louis Bonaparte," *Karl Marx: A Reader*, edited by Jon Elster, New York: Cambridge University Press, 1989, 277.
Miller, Arthur, *The Crucible*, Dramatists Play Service, Inc., 1982.
Nancy, Jean-Luc, *The Experience of Freedom*, translated by Bridget McDonald, Stanford, CA: Stanford University Press, 1993.
Shakespeare, *Hamlet*, New York: Methuen, 1982.

ONE

The Place That Is Not Here

Derrida's Africa and the Haunting of Place

Bruce B. Janz

Derrida foregrounds the question of place. One example comes from "Of the Humanities and the Philosophical Discipline: The Right to Philosophy from the Cosmopolitical Point of View (the Example of an International Institution)":

> I will begin with the question "where?"
> Not directly with the question "where are we?" or "where have we come to?" but "where does the question of the right to philosophy take place?," which can be immediately translated by "where ought it take place?"
> Where does it find today its most appropriate place?[1]

When most thinkers think Derrida on spatiality, their first thought is of *khōra*. When they think Derrida on platiality, on the other hand, they often think of Derrida's work on architecture and by extension questions about dwelling (Edward Casey's section on Derrida in *The Fate of Place* is a good example of this[2]). And, as is the case with the above quotation, thinking Derrida on the place of thought itself often leads to the place of the university, or the place of the humanities.

There is much rich material in these approaches, but if we want to understand something of Derrida's own places, they will help us less than it seems. Place is a specter, a haunting that does not easily fit with the Heideggerian notion of dwelling that has suffused so much discourse on place.[3] And, while thinking the place of thought is certainly a question about the constitution and shifting conditions of place, there is at the same time a kind of cosmopolitan implication to those discussions. It is rarely *this* university and *this* conversation in the humanities, whichever that may be, but the condition of the humanities in general. It is no accident that the touchstone for Derrida is Kant on this.[4]

Time and again, though, Derrida returns to places he has known. "Place" carries with it a phenomenological echo, a hint of yearning for authenticity and fixity, that makes it a strange concept to use in connection with Derrida. Did he not orient us toward deferral and openness by focusing on *khōra*? Doesn't "place" evoke all the things that Derrida was against, all the hints of ontotheology and logocentrism? And yet, he returns to place time and again, not just as a concept but as his own lived experience.

Perhaps the most sustained and evocative (although surely not the first) work that demonstrates the importance of Derrida's own places is Catherine Malabou's collection of and commentary on Derrida's work that has to do with travel, *Counterpath: Traveling with Jacques Derrida*.[5] Malabou reads Derrida as working out *khōra* in actual places, that is, as finding the spacing in which meaning and its lacks and deferrals can be theorized in the places to which he travels.

What is usually not done is to think Derrida's own place, his struggle with his own platiality as a creative act. For this, we must go to two places—his reflections on his own significant places, most notably Algeria,[6] but also France in general and Strasbourg, and then also his scattered comments about and engagement with Judaism. Malabou does this in *Counterpath*, of course, but there is more to be done. She is looking for *khōra*, for the ways in which thought finds its space to maneuver. I am interested in *lieu*, the return which catches Derrida up, the places that haunt him. This is not to say that *khōra*, architecture, and the university are not significant, but that in Derridean fashion to invert the usual order and ask the question of Derrida's own place will give us an opening not only to Derrida but also to larger questions of the postcolonial, the place of Africa, and the significance of concepts he leverages such as cosmopolitanism and hospitality. As has already been indicated, this also does not mean that place will stand as some fixity, through the means of cinders or haunting or mourning, which calls him back to some memory. That would be to misunderstand Derrida, but it would also be to misunderstand place.

The goal of this chapter is to think the ways in which Derrida addresses his own places, in particular Algeria. The goal is not to determine "what Algeria means to Derrida"—that would make no sense on Derrida's own terms. There is no lingering formative or causal influence of these past places that somehow explain anything. And, he did not treat these places from the past as if they were lingering presences waiting to be excavated. If we are waiting for some geographical determinism which could finally tell us what is African about Derrida, we will be disappointed. But nevertheless, his places matter. "A Judeo-Franco-Maghrebian genealogy does not clarify everything, far from it. But could I explain anything without it, ever?"[7] The question here is, in what manner do they matter for Derrida, and how does this way of facing place (yes, we will use the term, despite its baggage and the chance of misunderstanding it brings with it) tell us something new about place?

PLACE AND EVENT

Mark Wigley, in *The Architecture of Deconstruction*, focuses primarily on Derrida's implications for architecture, but in doing so he notes the ubiquitous nature of Derrida's concern with place:

> Derrida's essays are everywhere concerned with this question of place, or, rather, as he once put it, "the question of the enigma of place." There is no essay that doesn't at some point raise it, almost always literally as a question.[8]

Derrida's concern for place is not a yearning for presence but a question. Place is about displacement and disruption. What is true of architecture is just as true of other places he discusses.

Place as discussed in theoretical literature is sometimes taken as the given, the location in which things happen. This is in part an inheritance from Aristotle, the *locus* that establishes location and the *topos* which forms our topics and, as a result, our propositions. It comes too from a reductive and incorrect reading of Heidegger on dwelling, one which suggests a kind of Romantic rural scene which stands as authentic and is a true showing-forth of Being. Understood in these terms, place would seem like the very basis for logocentrism. And yet, this version of place might be seen, following Edward Casey, as "site," as a version of place that does not do justice to all that we mean to indicate when we talk about place. It is a version of place that does little more than apply a prior metaphysic to the material world.

Casey, in more recent work,[9] moves from places to edges, in particular in relation to Derrida, as (among other things) a way of extracting place from that kind of reductive and determinist reading that has become associated with it throughout the latter half of the twentieth century. One might, after all, read physical place with all the deconstructive skill that might be applied to any other text (and place is, after all, textualizable, whether or not it is a text[10]). There is, in other words, nothing inherently logocentric about place, any more than there is about any other text. It is the reading, rooted in a metaphysic, that renders it to be a site rather than a place. The point is to read against this version of place.

If deconstruction is a reading of the text which destabilizes it, showing forth its deferrals and lacunae, *khōra* is the reading of the place-text which does the same. It is, to be sure, more than that as well, but it is at least a way of facing specific place-texts, that deconstructs any claim to authenticity, and which instead offers a way of seeing the place-text as undecidable, as a virtuality.

Place, for Derrida, is event. This connection has been made before, in Heidegger's *Ereignis* (see, for instance, Jeff Malpas's unpacking of this in *Heidegger's Topology*[11]). Event is a concept used by many, both within the phenomenological tradition and also by those skeptical of it (e.g., Badiou, Deleuze). And, Derrida uses it, at least to think through the "impossible possibility of saying the event."[12] Michael Marder works out a theory of the event in Derrida's later work as well, which focusses on things, but which is also relevant to the place as I have described it here. It is a double movement, "place without place."[13]

In other words, as we look at how Derrida treats place throughout his work, we are led to where he always leads us, to displacement, and to the deferral of place. Place is not simply about containers in space, but about events that have happened and could happen. When it comes to his own places, one might even say it is about "learning to live finally."

Derrida does, in fact, directly connect place and event, even as he recognizes the mysterious nature of place:

> What strikes me when the question you raise is centered around the question of place is a certain type of deconstructive thinking, at least the kind that has interested me personally more and more for some time now: that is, precisely, the question and the enigma of event as that which takes place [qui a lieu], the question of the enigma of place. And here we have to proceed very, very slowly and very, very cautiously when we ask ourselves what we really mean by place. Thinking about the question of place is a very difficult thing—as is thinking about event as something which takes place. It's finally a question of the topikos in the rhetorical sense, as a localizing of what comes to pass in the sense of event, of Ereignis. My reference to Heidegger is often a reference to those places in Heidegger's thought where the question of place is very alive and very mysterious too. All this means that the question of place is absolutely essential, but all the more difficult to circumscribe and to isolate.[14]

While his version of place does not have the element of presencing we find in Heidegger's dwelling, it is clear that *Ereignis* does have some resonance for Derrida. It is possible, in other words, to have place without presencing, and that is what Derrida is interested in exploring, and what calls him back to Algeria and other places.

DERRIDA'S PLACES

Derrida uses the language of dwelling when speaking about language, and in particular when speaking about language in the context of his relationship to Algeria. He even speaks of "dwelling":

> "My monolingualism dwells, and I call it my dwelling; it feels like one to me, and I remain in it and inhabit it. It inhabits me. ... Yes, I have only one language, yet it is not mine.[15]

The dwelling of language is the place I have sketched out to this point. It is a statement about language in general, and postcolonialism, and Derrida's relationship to Fanon and others in Algeria,[16] and yet it is also about his own place, his place without place.

Re-orienting place opens the door to consider the many passages in which Derrida speaks of his own place-texts, as well as the ways in which he speaks of Algeria, Strasbourg, and other places. None of these are anchored, and yet, he returns to them, literally and figuratively. It is never about establishing some sort of echo of the site of past action. Perhaps the way of understanding why place might matter is to think about the other alternatives, if retrieving an echo is not the point in facing a particular past. What other options might there be in relating to the particular or platial past? We could, for one thing, try to invent the platial past, that is, we could try to impose our will upon the particularities of the place. We could make specific places look like we want. In that invented place, the past has no hold on us, but we have a hold on it.

There is plenty of evidence, though, that such a strategy is unrealistic. Foucault shows us that, while all history might be history of the present, that does not mean that we anachronistically impose the will of the present on the past. It merely means that we have no access to that past without asking about the contemporary frame that motivates it.

We could, secondly, simply choose to ignore the past. We might just think that history is bunk, as Henry Ford said, and we could strive to create a future. But this too seems unrealistic—we are more likely back in the first untenable option of inventing a past, since despite what Ford might have thought, we never actually extract ourselves out of the material and intellectual spaces that were created before.

We could, thirdly, perspectivize the particular past. In other words, we could regard the past as subject to individual memory and narrative. This way of thinking about particular platial past throws the question of meaning back onto the subject without in any way interrogating what that subject is. The subject just is its perspective.

The point is this—Derrida is not taking any of these superficial stances toward the particular platial past. He continually returns to the questions of the places of his past, but not to ask about the hold they have on us, nor to imaginatively create them, nor to simply deny them and move on, nor to relativize them. They have another place, but he continually returns to those places. He raises the question of Algeria over and over again. He thinks about it in relation to his Sephardic Jewishness, in relation to language and writing, in relation to hospitality and friendship. These particular places keep returning in him, as him. His place-texts are ever-present in his thoughts, even if not as presence.

As he says, for him, "chora [*khōra*] would situate the abstract spacing, *place itself* the place of absolute exteriority, but also the place of a bifurcation between two approaches to the desert,"[17] so that what emerges is a new register, something closer to a lived place. It is his place, to be sure, his place as activated by language, as made available by being outside of his only language. But it is not only his place, but the potentiality of place. We see the contrast between his reflection on places that have history or emotion for him (Algeria, Strasbourg) and those which do not have that kind of background (for instance, in his engagement with South Africa[18]). The former are questioned differently than the latter, which is not to say that he presents South Africa in simplified terms (he explicitly says that he will not do that), but that South Africa is engaged mainly as a juridical and political space, not as a space that haunts him in the manner that Algeria does.

And yet, throughout *Monolingualism* we have the sense of a specific place brought back to Derrida in a manner that was not apparent earlier. We might see a similar grappling with his Jewish past at the same time. We see him engage with significant places, such as Strasbourg, which gives him the opportunity to reflect on Algeria, and even speak about his "Strasbourgian nostalgia."[19]

We see, in other words, what it means to take place (that is, to happen or occur), to replace and displace, to find and lose place, to stand in place of the other, and ultimately to face the placeless place. Place becomes event; in an inversion of Michel de Certeau's "space is practiced place" dictum, for Derrida place is the event of space and time. Derrida, in his "Provocation" to *Without Alibi* links place, alibi, and the trace:

> [O]ne must also recall something obvious concerning the ordinary usage of the word "alibi," its pragmatic meaning, therefore, which is always more forceful and determining than the neutral semantics of the lexicon. According to this lexicon, in the slumber of dictionaries, "alibi" means simply "elsewhere," "in another place [*alius ibi*]." But no one ever uses the adverb, and it is never translated into a substantive—"the alibi," "an alibi"—except in situations where the alibi is, in good or bad faith, veraciously or mendaciously, alleged in order to disculpate (oneself), justify (oneself) in the course of an investigation, an accusation, or a trial. The allegation of an alibi always has the form of a plea for the defense. It acquires meaning only in an experience that puts into play an incrimination, accusation, guilt, and thus responsibility (judicial or penal, but first of all ethical or political). Hence the most

> general question: Can one speak of an alibi, of an experience of referral to an elsewhere, to another (another place, another moment, another "who" or "what") before this scene of culpa-responsibility, of duty or debt (Schuld, Schuldigsein)? If one thinks, as I was suggesting above, that every trace secretes some alibi, will it be possible to think the trace, and thus the alibi, in a neutral fashion, before the proceedings of culpa-responsibility? Or is the injunction to answer (to answer to, to answer for, and so forth) inscribed right on the trace?[20]

The alibi is elsewhere, another place, a place of responsibility, a debt. It is the placeless place of the ancestors. And yet the ancestors are *of* some place, of which they bear the trace.

WHAT DOES IT MEAN TO THINK A PLACE? BEING HAUNTED BY THE ANCESTORS

While Derrida uses the word "place" regularly, his thinking of place is not limited to his own place-texts (or for that matter, to *khōra*). He is thinking place when he thinks about limits, and aporias. Place, for him, is haunted—specters speak to the aporias in place, to the events that bring together thought, action, and history. Recall that place is event—these specters are not just anchors to a past, but the opportunity to write place anew. It is not no-place or imaginary place, but placeless place. This is how places are haunted.

The Mahgreb, then, is a place in this sense, in the sense of an aporia, a haunting, a virtuality. We can see that haunting in his work—he regularly returns to the subject of Algeria, sometimes telling the same stories over again, about how he lost his citizenship and then regained it, about the place of language. It is as if he must speak back to the specters, not to assert an identity as Algerian or African or even French, but to ask them what new event they might have for him, as he thinks Algeria in light of other questions and other imperatives which press upon him. Living with the dead is, after all, a condition of living:

> "Living together," with the dead, is not an accident, a miracle, or an extraordinary story [histoire]. It is rather an essential possibility of existence. It reminds us that in "living together" the idea of life is neither simple nor dominant even if it remains irreducible.[21]

Specters are not, of course, merely the dead that have gone before, but they are part of that haunting, the memory of living together but also the gaps and deferrals of that memory. These specters are like the ancestors we might find in some versions of traditional African philosophy. They are *genius loci*, spirits of the place that come back, bidden or not, to remind him that the place of Algeria is neither an originary set of meanings coded into his being and waiting to be uncovered, nor an assertion of the will, nor a utopian place. Haunting is not a spectral presence, a mystical or ghostly power. These ancestors are judges, not in the sense of those who enforce a pre-existing moral code but in the sense of those who call forth the force of law. As such they are also those who give the basis for hospitality, inviting us to a place while at the same time setting the patterns and practices of the place, at some uncanny level. Algeria haunts Derrida as ancestors do in some traditions of African thought. It would be the wrong question to ask whether or in what form these ancestors exist. This is not the register of metaphysics, which is where so much African philosophy has started in its formative decades. It is not the "presence of a dead ancestor in the living Ego," as Nicholas Abraham and Maria Torok might say.[22] It is rather the recognition that ancestors haunt their specific cultures and places as absence, not presence, as the death which is ever-present in life.

"A specter is haunting Europe"—it is not haunting a person but a place-text. Derrida speaks most famously about the specters of Marx, and in the book of that title brings mourning to the foreground.[23] Mourning is not just memory, but the recognition of haunting, of the waft of smoke from cinders. It is the recognition that something is within us, whether we can articulate it or not, and that what is in us is a negation. Derrida's *The Work of Mourning*[24] is potentially misleading, as we might be inclined to link mourning to the loss of a specific friend at a specific time. But mourning is much more than that. Mourning changes us. Living is mourning—we always owe to others who came before. Mourning is the space of the ancestors, of the time within that is "given" to us, by history, by our claim on that which was and still is within us.

> It's true; attention to a certain spectral logic, almost everywhere, seems to be taking a remarkably insistent form these days. It is thus, of course, essentially connected to the question of the technical prosthesis, of technics in general, of the inevitability of the work of mourning—which is not one work among others but the overdetermining mark of all work. It also concerns the impossibility of mourning. Mourning must be impossible. Successful mourning is failed mourning. In successful mourning, I incorporate the one who has died, I assimilate him to myself, I reconcile myself with death, and consequently I deny death and the alterity of the dead other and of death as other. I am therefore unfaithful. Where the introjection of mourning succeeds, mourning annuls the other. I take him upon me, and consequently I negate or delimit his infinite alterity.[25]

"Ancestor" has received remarkably little attention in African philosophy for a concept which has such clear relevance to social philosophy and morality. Most of what can be found is by Western anthropologists, and so the interest is often more ethnographic than philosophical. If the ancestor is seen as the haunting of a place and a people, though, it becomes philosophically interesting. The Nigerian philosopher Bartholomew Abanuka is one of the few who has written about ancestors.[26] Despite focusing initially on the metaphysics of ancestors (where do they exist in relation to the material world and to the absolute?), he spends most of his time thinking about their function. He emphasizes their presence, specifically the ways in which they reinforce a moral and social order. We might think, then, that they do not haunt in Derrida's sense, as an uncanny sense. But they do haunt African culture. They are not simply principles of moral order, but exemplars and echoes and revenant elements that animate and establish place (understood here as community).

And so, ancestors are mourned, but mourning is not simply sadness at the loss of someone or something. Mourning is a wound, a *stigmē*, that which is left behind after wounding, "in (the) place of this event, place is given over, for the same wound, to substitution, which repeats itself there, retaining of the irreplaceable only a past desire."[27] Hélène Cixous says that she and Derrida have "in common a number of precise and dated stigmata: Algeria 1940."[28] The stigmata, the wound left after the sharp point has been removed, allows the ancestor to haunt us and allows the cinders to linger and be acknowledged. It is the establishment of place by allowing the *genius loci* to take place, not as a presence but as a substitution, an absence that creates a wound. Derrida theorized mourning in the act of mourning his departed friends. In his memorial to Barthes, he speaks about Barthes' own ancestors:

> The deaths of Roland Barthes: *his* deaths, that is, those of his relatives, those deaths that must have inhabited him, situating places and solemn moments, orienting tombs in his inner space (ending—and probably even beginning—with his mother's death). *His* deaths, those he lived in the plural, those he must have linked together, trying in vain to "dialectize" them before the "total" and "undialectical" death; those deaths that always form in our lives a terrifying and endless series.[29]

Barthes' imperative of engaging these deaths drove him, Derrida argues, to a *punctum*, an instant in time and place that "rends space." For Barthes the *punctum* is mediated by the photograph (in *Camera Lucida*), and Derrida frames the photograph as follows:

> Though it is no longer *there* (present, living, real), its *having-been-there* presently a part of the referential or intentional structure of my relationship to the photogram, the return of the referent indeed takes the form of a haunting. This is a "return of the dead," whose spectral arrival in the very space of the photogram indeed resembles that of an emission or emanation. Already a sort of hallucinating metonymy: it is something else, a piece come from the other (from the referent) that finds itself in me, before me, but also in me like a piece of me (since the referential implication is also intentional and noematic; it belongs neither to the sensible body nor to the medium of the photogram).[30]

Derrida notes that Barthes's conclusion from this is that "I have become Total-Image, which is to say, Death in person." Death is not simply the static capture of the image, taking it out of time, but the engagement and production of a haunting, a struggle with the ancestors and an entry into ancestor-hood ourselves.

Ancestors are sometimes seen as morally and culturally conservative elements within an African moral order. They are seen as the part of the community that ensures fealty to a past moral order, and are sometimes used as a call to return to a different social state in the face of corruption in society and other problems of modernism. When they are imagined as these conservative elements, they end up being a kind of proxy for contemporary concerns, usually those of waning traditional power structures. They buttress an order that is perceived as being lost. They are, as described before, a reading-back into the particular place of the past. And yet, it is not clear that the role of moral proxy remains true to the social role of ancestors. Kwame Gyekye famously argued that tradition is not what is handed down, but what is taken on by a younger generation.[31] This "taking on" need not be seen as just a form of extracting usable history (that would be to privilege the younger generation at the expense of the older), but following Michael Naas can be something more like taking on a tradition in all its mystery and contradiction.[32] It is not necessarily the rational or pragmatic decision of a younger generation at the smorgasbord of history. Taking on might be a kind of haunting by the past, by the ancestors who are not present to enforce an abstract sense of order but to raise questions. The real question here is, can the understanding of ancestors be seen to open place to new questions and new forms of life, rather than close place down and use it as the imposition of a specific will?

For Derrida, haunting is about ultimate owing and duty. It is not that ancestors are just moral guides, they are the space of thought for Africa. They demand that we narrate the past. They inhabit the narratives of place, along with tales and proverbs, and yet they are not nuggets of eternal wisdom. They are invitations, the spaces to think about what it means to live in those places, the ones that are still alive despite the smell of death on them.[33]

TWO FORMS OF ANTI-COLONIALISM

We are ready to return to the Mahgreb. Place-texts clearly lie in the ever-present haunting of the ancestors, and Derrida, for his part, returns time and again to Algeria.

The question remains as to how these places are or can be written. John Protevi suggests two ways, represented by Derrida and Deleuze:

> Derrida's work, though destroying the self-evidence of the various identification machines at work today—the naturalized self-images of nations, races, genders, subjects and so on—by inscribing the produc-

tion of meaning in a world of 'force and signification,' can only prepare the way for the radicality of Deleuzean historical—libidinal materialism: the principles guiding the empirical study of forceful bodies politic in their material production.[34]

Derrida's orientation to place is different from Heidegger's. Heidegger continually looks for the traces of dwelling, the originary state that grounds meaning. He looks for Being. Derrida focusses on the negation, absence (in this sense he looks back to Hegel). His places are haunted, by the no-longer and the not-yet, by the placeless place. His places are uncanny, and they are the reason that we mourn. The more personal they get, the more that Derrida grapples with the ghosts of his own Algeria, the more opening there is for writing Algeria.

Deleuze gives a different complexion to place. There is neither the yearning for the originary, nor is there a haunting, but rather, an affirmation. All three, Heidegger, Derrida, and Deleuze, look back to Nietzsche, but Deleuze has the most direct debt. It is the debt of becoming.

What might this mean? For one thing, we might follow up Derrida's insight from "Racism's Last Word" that "there is no racism without a language,"[35] but take it in a different direction. This place, these ancestors, might point to the ways in which concepts are activated. There is no racism without language, yes, and there is in fact no race without language. And, it may be that we might move toward "a thousand tiny races,"[36] even as we can perform a thousand tiny sexes. Whereas Deleuze points us toward the creation of new concepts and the activation of ecosystems of thought, Derrida reminds us of the ancestors, the words that can never be said in that creation and activation. Within Deleuze and Guattari's minoritarian literature[37] that writes a new Algeria and a new Africa, that resists the molar politics with the molecular, the ancestors still remain. This is understood perhaps most immediately in the fact that justice is never accomplished and equality is never a task that we can move beyond. To Deleuze's radically creative sense of becoming, the ancestors are still needed. To be sure, this is something most Deleuzians would likely resist. The point here, though, is that the places we find ourselves in are both places of new creation and places of haunting by ancestors. Derrida points us to the placeless place of place-texts, the "in *lieu* of," the lack or the other, and at the same time, Deleuze points us to deterritorialization and reterritorialization. To lose either of these is to reduce our places to something less, something utilitarian, nostalgic, coercive, or ideal.

What is Derrida's direction on the question of the resistance to colonialism? Catherine Malabou summarizes it best:

> Every Monolingualism and monologism restores mastery or magistrality. It is by *treating* each language *differently*, by *grafting* languages onto one another, by *playing* on the multiplicity of languages and on the

multiplicity of codes within every linguistic corpus that we can struggle at once against *colonization* in general, against the colonizing principle in general (and you know that it exerts itself well beyond the zones said to be subjected to colonization), against the domination of language or domination by language.[38]

And so we see two directions for resisting colonialism between Derrida and Deleuze. For Derrida, it is to go inside the language and the code to see the ways in which it is never one but many, never unified but manipulated. For Deleuze, it is to go between languages, to create a minoritarian literature, which is not a move to show the fissures within language itself but a move to create anew a way of speaking by seeing languages always as dialects, always as place-bound. It is to stutter, that is, to hesitate, procrastinate, to be in doubt, and to hold the self as a question.

This is not a contrast between one thinker who attends to a version of place and another that does not. As I have argued, Derrida is haunted in a particular way by place-texts. It is consistent with the generative space of *khōra*, but it has a very different, much more personal feel. It is Derrida implicated by his own place, Algeria, as well as his Jewish place, and the places he loves, such as Strasbourg. While both Deleuze and Derrida resist Heidegger, they are also both children of Heidegger, but in different ways. For Deleuze, the debt is a refrain that produces a virtuality in the form of a new direction in the production of place. A minoritarian literature does more to produce place than the exercise of will on the part of the molar state. For Derrida, on the other hand, as much as Heidegger is deconstructed, it is as if Derrida takes us past Heidegger's notion of dwelling. For Heidegger there seem to be few resources for the resistance of something like colonialism (and perhaps even a predisposition toward the authenticity of a place and its people that has more in common with the aspirations of the *Blut und Boden* of National Socialism than anything else). There is none of this with Derrida. The specters are uncanny. His return to his places is not the return to fixed points which can serve as orientation markers, but the return to the wound, the stigmata, evidence of placeless place and the call to write again. All of which makes, ironically, all (his) writing a striving for, and in, place.

CONCLUSION

Derrida finishes "Of the Humanities and the Philosophical Discipline" with this, in response to a long quotation from Kant's *Idea for a Universal History from a Cosmopolitical Point of View*:

> With this citation I wanted to suggest that the right to philosophy may require from now on a distinction among several registers of debt, between a finite debt and an infinite debt, between debt and duty,

between a certain erasure and a certain reaffirmation of debt and sometimes a certain erasure in the name of reaffirmation.[39]

These debts are what mourning is about, that is, the encounter with the ancestors. And, it is part of what draws Derrida back to Algeria time and again. He has a debt. That debt is not always clear (it is half-heard and uncanny), but it keeps coming up, over and over again in his later writings. The impetus is not one of the determination of identity. No one who has read him at all would expect him to be asking for anything stable. Any question of whether he "really" Algerian, French, or Jewish is immaterial. What is material is that there is a force that necessitates questioning, and an awareness of absence, that is, a haunting.

"Der Ort sagt," Derrida says.[40] He was speaking of Strasbourg, but in some sense every place that haunts him speaks. In the end, it is *khōra*, yes, but perhaps the specters of the Algeria are what allow his places to speak to him. Can they speak beyond him? Surely they can, inasmuch as their speaking is an event, a particularly powerful haunting that remains with us because it remained with him.[41]

NOTES

1. Jacques Derrida, "Of the Humanities and the Philosophical Discipline: The Right to Philosophy from the Cosmopolitical Point of View (the Example of an International Institution)" *Surfaces* Vol. IV. 310 Folio 1 (1994), Montréal. Accessed December 9, 2015. http://www.pum.umontreal.ca/revues/surfaces/vol4/derridaa.html. Essay reprinted in Derrida, *Ethics, Institutions, and the Right to Philosophy*, (Lanham, MD: Rowman & Littlefield), 2002.
2. Edward Casey, *The Fate of Place: A Philosophical History*, (Berkeley: University of California Press, 1997), 309–321.
3. For more, see John Wylie, "The Spectral Geographies of W. G. Sebald" in *Cultural Geographies* 14 (2007): 171–188.
4. For examples, see Jacques Derrida, "Mochlos, or, the Conflict of the Faculties" in Rand, Richard, ed., *Logomachia: The Conflict of the Faculties*, (Lincoln: University of Nebraska Press, 1992), 1–34.
5. Jacques Derrida and Catherine Malabou, *Counterpath*, (Stanford: Stanford University Press, 2004).
6. See, for example, Jacques Derrida, "Taking a Stand for Algeria" in *Acts of Religion*, (London: Routledge, 2002), 301–308.
7. Jacques Derrida, *Monolingualism of the Other; or, The Prosthesis of Origin*, (Stanford: Stanford University Press, 1998), 71–72.
8. Mark Wigley, *The Architecture of Deconstruction: Derrida's Haunt*, (Boston: MIT Press, 1997), 177–78.
9. Edward Casey, "Going to the Edge" in *The Oxford Literary Review* 36:2 (2014): 191–195.
10. For more on this, see Bruce Janz, "Is Place a Text?" in Bruce B. Janz, ed. *Place, Space and Hermeneutics*, (New York: Springer, 2017), 23–34.
11. Jeff Malpas, *Heidegger's Topology*, (Boston: MIT Press, 2006), 211ff.
12. Jacques Derrida, *Learning to Live Finally: The Last Interview*, (London: Palgrave Macmillan, 2007).
13. Michael Marder, *The Event of the Thing: Derrida's Post-Deconstructive Realism*, (Toronto: University of Toronto Press, 2009), 17.

14. Jacques Derrida with James Creech, Peggy Kamuf and Jane Todd, "Deconstruction in America: An Interview with Jacques Derrida" in *Critical Exchange* 17 (Winter 1985), 4–5.

15. Derrida, *Monolingualism*, 1–2.

16. Grant Farred, "'Nostalgeria': Derrida, Before and After Fanon" in *The South Atlantic Quarterly* 112:1 (Winter 2013), 145–162.

17. Jacques Derrida, "Faith and Knowledge" in *Acts of Religion*, (London: Routledge, 2002), 57.

18. Jacques Derrida, "Racism's Last Word" in *Signature Derrida*, (Chicago: University of Chicago Press), 2013.

19. Jacques Derrida, *For Strasbourg: Conversations of Friendship and Philosophy*, (New York: Fordham University Press, 2014), 7.

20. Jacques Derrida, *Without Alibi*, (Stanford: Stanford University Press, 2002), xxvi-xxvii.

21. Jacques Derrida, "Avowing—The Impossible: "Returns," Repentance, and Reconciliation," E. Weber, ed., *Living Together: Jacques Derrida's Communities of Violence and Peace*, (New York: Fordham University Press, 2012), 20.

22. Colin Davis, "État Présent: Hauntology, Spectres and Phantoms" in *French Studies* 59:3 (2005), 374. See also Jacques Derrida, "Fors: The Anglish Words of Nicolas Abraham and Maria Torok" in *The Georgia Review* 31:1 (Spring 1977), 64–116.

23. Jacques Derrida, *Specters of Marx*, (London: Routledge, 1994).

24. Jacques Derrida, *The Work of Mourning*, (Chicago: University of Chicago Press, 2001).

25. Jacques Derrida and Elisabeth Roudinesco, *For What Tomorrow…A Dialogue*, (Stanford: Stanford University Press, 2004), 159–160.

26. Bartholomew Abanuka, *A New Essay in African Philosophy*, (Nsukka Nigeria: Spiritan Publications, 1994).

27. Derrida, *The Work of Mourning*, 67.

28. Hélène Cixous, *Portrait of Jacques Derrida as a Young Jewish Saint*, (New York: Columbia University Press, 2004), x.

29. Derrida, *The Work of Mourning*, 52.

30. Derrida, *The Work of Mourning*, 54.

31. Kwame Gyekye, *Tradition and Modernity: Philosophical Reflections on the African Experience*, (Oxford: Oxford University Press, 1997), 221ff.

32. Michael Naas, *Taking On the Tradition: Jacques Derrida and the Legacies of Deconstruction*, (Stanford: Stanford University Press, 2003).

33. Achille Mbembe, *On the Postcolony*. (University of California Press, 2001).

34. John Protevi, *Political Physics: Deleuze Derrida and the Body Politics*, (London and New York: Athlone Press, 2001), 2.

35. Derrida, "Racism's Last Word," 54.

36. Arun Saldanha, "Reontologising Race: The Machinic Geography of Phenotype" in *Environment and Planning D: Society and Space* 24 (2006), 9–24.

37. Gilles Deleuze and Felix Guattari, *Kafka: Toward a Minor Literature*, (Minneapolis: University of Minnesota Press, 1986).

38. Derrida and Malabou, *Counterpath*, 89.

39. Derrida, "Of the Humanities and the Philosophical Discipline," 16–17.

40. Derrida, *For Strasbourg*, 1.

41. Thanks to Peter Gratton and Sabatino DiBernardo for comments on an earlier draft of this chapter, as well as to the comments by participants in the Cornell workshop "Jacques Derrida: A Figure of African Thought" in April of 2016, hosted by Grant Farred.

WORKS CITED

Abanuka, Bartholomew. *A New Essay in African Philosophy*. Nsukka Nigeria: Spiritan Publications, 1994.
Casey, Edward. *The Fate of Place: A Philosophical History*. Berkeley: University of California Press, 1997.
Casey, Edward. "Going to the Edge" in *The Oxford Literary Review* 36:2 (2014): 191–195.
Cixous, Hélène. *Portrait of Jacques Derrida as a Young Jewish Saint*. New York: Columbia University Press, 2004.
Davis, Colin. "État Présent: Hauntology, Spectres and Phantoms" in *French Studies* 59:3 (2005): 373–379.
Deleuze, Gilles and Felix Guattari, *Kafka: Toward a Minor Literature*. Minneapolis: University of Minnesota Press, 1986.
Derrida, Jacques. "Avowing—The Impossible: "Returns," Repentance, and Reconciliation." E. Weber, ed. *Living Together: Jacques Derrida's Communities of Violence and Peace*. New York: Fordham University Press, 2012: 18–41.
Derrida, Jacques. "A Certain Impossible Possibility of Saying the Event" in *Critical Inquiry* 33 (Winter 2007): 441–461.
Derrida, Jacques. "The Crisis in the Teaching of Philosophy" in *Who's Afraid of Philosophy? Right to Philosophy 1*. Stanford: Stanford University Press, 2002: 99–116.
Derrida, Jacques. "Faith and Knowledge" in *Acts of Religion*. London: Routledge, 2002: 42–101.
Derrida, Jacques. *For Strasbourg: Conversations of Friendship and Philosophy*. New York: Fordham University Press, 2014.
Derrida, Jacques. "Fors: The Anglish Words of Nicolas Abraham and Maria Torok" in *The Georgia Review* 31:1 (Spring 1977): 64–116.
Derrida, Jacques. *Learning to Live Finally: The Last Interview*. Palgrave Macmillan, 2007.
Derrida, Jacques. "Mochlos, or, the Conflict of the Faculties" in Rand, Richard, ed., *Logomachia: The Conflict of the Faculties*. Lincoln: University of Nebraska Press, 1992: 1–34.
Derrida, Jacques. *Monolingualism of the Other; or, The Prosthesis of Origin*. Stanford: Stanford University Press, 1998.
Derrida, Jacques. "Of the Humanities and the Philosophical Discipline: The Right to Philosophy from the Cosmopolitical Point of View (the Example of an International Institution)" *Surfaces* Vol. IV. 310 Folio 1 (1994), Montréal. Accessed December 9, 2015. http://www.pum.umontreal.ca/revues/surfaces/vol4/derridaa.html Essay reprinted in Derrida, *Ethics, Institutions, and the Right to Philosophy*. Lanham, MD: Rowman & Littlefield, 2002.
Derrida, Jacques. "Racism's Last Word" in *Signature Derrida*. Chicago: University of Chicago Press, 2013.
Derrida, Jacques. *Specters of Marx*. London: Routledge, 1994.
Derrida, Jacques. "Taking a Stand for Algeria" in *Acts of Religion*. London: Routledge, 2002: 301–308.
Derrida, Jacques. *Without Alibi*. Stanford: Stanford University Press, 2002.
Derrida, Jacques. *The Work of Mourning*. Chicago: University of Chicago Press, 2001.
Derrida, Jacques & Catherine Malabou. *Counterpath*. Stanford: Stanford University Press, 2004.
Derrida, Jacques & Elisabeth Roudinesco. *For What Tomorrow…A Dialogue*. Stanford: Stanford University Press, 2004.
Derrida, Jacques and Hélène Cixous. "From the Word to Life: A Dialogue Between Jacques Derrida and Hélène Cixous" *New Literary History* 2005: 1–13.
Derrida, Jacques with James Creech, Peggy Kamuf and Jane Todd. "Deconstruction in America: An Interview with Jacques Derrida" in *Critical Exchange* 17 (Winter 1985): 1–33.
Farred, Grant. "'Nostalgeria': Derrida, Before and After Fanon" in *The South Atlantic Quarterly* 112:1 (Winter 2013): 145–162.

Gyekye, Kwame. *Tradition and Modernity: Philosophical Reflections on the African Experience*. Oxford: Oxford University Press, 1997.

Janz, Bruce. "Debt and Duty: Kant, Derrida, and African Philosophy," Special issue of *Janus Head*, Winter 2001. Available at: http://www.janushead.org/gwu-2001/janz.cfm.

Janz, Bruce, "Is Place a Text?" in Bruce B. Janz, ed. *Place, Space and Hermeneutics*. New York: Springer, 2017: 23–34.

Malpas, Jeff. *Heidegger's Topology*. Boston: MIT Press, 2006.

Marder, Michael. *The Event of the Thing: Derrida's Post-Deconstructive Realism*. Toronto: University of Toronto Press, 2009.

Naas, Michael. *Taking On the Tradition: Jacques Derrida and the Legacies of Deconstruction*. Stanford: Stanford University Press, 2003.

Protevi, John. *Political Physics: Deleuze Derrida and the Body Politics*. London and New York: Athlone Press, 2001.

Saldanha, Arun. "Reontologising Race: The Machinic Geography of Phenotype" in *Environment and Planning D: Society and Space* 24 (2006): 9–24.

Weber, Elisabeth. "Living—with—Torture—Together" in E. Weber, ed. *Living Together: Jacques Derrida's Communities of Violence and Peace*. New York: Fordham University Press, 2012: 243–248.

Wigley, Mark. *The Architecture of Deconstruction: Derrida's Haunt*. Boston: MIT Press, 1997.

Wylie, John. "The Spectral Geographies of W. G. Sebald" in *Cultural Geographies* 14 (2007): 171–188.

TWO

Deconstruction as Diaspora

On Derrida, Africa, and Identity's Deferral

John E. Drabinski

WHAT IS DERRIDA TO AFRICA? AND WHAT IS AFRICA TO DERRIDA?

This reversal raises a biographical question, perhaps, and as such gives us very little for thinking. If we simply wonder about Derrida's Africanness *as a person* and as a person *in relation to this land*, then we already ask the wrong questions. Geography and origin, transparency to self and language—this is already something(s) that Derrida himself has shown to be colonial in motivation and imagination. And yet, there is the autobiographical moment. What is Africa to Derrida as he imagines himself, a self in the deconstructed time-space of identification, fractured and scattered, yet compelled to conjugate being, the neutral to-be, into the first person? We have an answer to this, or at least address it as a provocation. Derrida conjugates his identity, and maybe also the identity of deconstruction as theoretical space, in a well-known passage from "The Crisis of Teaching," uttering or writing the phrase "the sort of uprooted African I am."[1] As a kind of performative utterance, the enactment of speaking or a speaking, Derrida's declaration of Africanness can be read as not so much a description of a reality in his biography—though it is certainly that—but rather as a fundamental shift in the social and cultural meaning of "Derrida," Derridean anti- and ante-thinking, and indeed deconstruction itself. Or at least this is what I want to suggest. The uprooted African who Derrida *is* becomes that African, becomes Derrida and deconstruction, and *becomes the unrooted* in the very moment of its utterance.

The African who Derrida is, however, remains suspended between what we might imagine to be Africa and what we know to have been (and still be) the violence in Africa: the colonized and the colonizer. "[B]orn in Algeria," Derrida writes, "in an environment about which it will always be difficult to say whether it was colonized or colonizing."[2] This birthplace is both senses of uprooted at once. The uprooted as a *people* constituted by dislocation and loss (and all the more that comes *after* dislocation) *and* the uprooting as a people who are marked by the enacting of violence against them. This suspension of place or reconfiguration of location as the convergence of contrary times in one space—the time of the colonizing and the colonized in Algeria or the Maghreb more widely—marks Derrida's being, the conjugation into the *am* and, for us, the *is*, with undecidability, fracture, and the simultaneity of impossibility (the loss sustained by the colonized) and various forms of possibility, both violent (colonizing) and something very different (the survival of the colonized inside and after violence). The uprooted African that Derrida *is* is therefore always, for Derrida and even deconstruction itself, a fundamentally diasporic body, method, and paradox of identity.

Rather than the complexity of Derrida's biography and autobiography (if such a distinction obtains) or the peculiar questions of the place of the Maghreb in the imagination of Africa, the following reflections want to tell a story of deconstruction as a theory of diaspora. Or, perhaps better, a story of diaspora as already the story of deconstruction, something that helps us understand—and I will return to this at the close—how monolingualism can be violence, dwelling, and a modality of being, knowing, and doing while *also* registering all of those contraries in erasure, in the blindness of memoir, and in the failure to come to terms and into language rooted in the security rooted history. How, then, does Derrida's utterance "the uprooted African I am" open up a conception of deconstruction as a theory of diaspora and theorizing diaspora as theorizing the possibility of deconstruction? Perhaps deconstruction is impossible without uprooted Africans, by which I mean, perhaps the dislocation of the African initiates deconstruction and presents deconstruction to itself in that moment of dislocation, then initiation. Impossible without Derrida the Algerian, the African, the dislocated Maghreb wanderer between the colonized and the intractability of colonizing force.

Again: ". . . the uprooted African that I am." I want to come back to this phrase three times below in order to explore and spatial and temporal registers of the utterance. As a critical concept, the phrase functions something like a supplement, an addition to what we *know* about Derrida (the Greekjew who, like Levinas, is also Jewgreek) that is no mere additive, but, instead, a decisive turn and twist, from the margins, inside the very notion of identity. In this way, the supplement does not and can never twist free, even as an aspirational orientation; here, as is perhaps familiar at this point, the difference between Heidegger's destruction of the history of philosophy (of Being) and the early Derrida's conception of deconstruction as *différance* is crucial. Heidegger's de-structuring of the history of philosophy destabilizes all of the texts as he moves through the Occident, exposing the dependence of the tradition on certain conceptions of presence and absence, and yet the aim, in the end, is a retrieval of the word or words for Being that bring the work of truth as presencing into view. Derrida's deconstruction has no such aim. Destabilization is not a strategy. It is, rather, a feature of what we call, alternately, sites, worlds, places, spaces, and times. The dislocated African does not hearken back to presencing or truth, but rather initiates *différance* in the uprooted African Derrida *is*. The phrase and its function as a supplement is therefore the *story* and *history* of deconstruction, and so, as we shall see, is also the story and history of a certain kind of diaspora.

What follows, then, is something of an exploration. An exploration of the African that Derrida *is* as the site of reflection on the meaning of diaspora and deconstruction. What remains of either, and with what each might respond insofar as any distance is possible, hinges in part on the meaning of roots and uprootedness. Roots and uprootedness, as the ground of diasporic and deconstructive thinking, twist and turn in order to dismantle, then register loss and mourning, and then, having twisted, turned, lost, and mourned, live on despite it all. Perhaps that is the story of the African Derrida: uprooted, constituted by loss, and yet he who dwells, he who seeks dwelling in that complicated sense of dwelling we find in *Monolingualism of the Other* and elsewhere.

MONOAFRICA

A Turning and Twisting, Then, as a First Register.

Uprooting is constitutive of deconstructive space as an anti-spatiality. Spatiality is undone, unraveled, and dismantled by the infusion of a radical temporality—a sense of time that does not obey the laws of physics or the economy of retrieval and inheritance. But temporality is no different; the flow of time is already spatialized. This insight is formulated in the "Différance" essay in the straightforward and reversible "*Différance* as temporalization, *différance* as spatialization,"[3] a formulation that I would argue operates as a transcendental across Derrida's work. The conceptual work of grammatology, the *pharmakon*, and so on, as well as the concrete, provocative work of justice, hospitality, and perhaps even autoimmunity, all turn on the reversibility of temporality and spatiality. *Différance*, in that sense, functions as a transcendental structure that conditions the possibility of the life and death of language, of drawing the boundary and transgressing it, and of marking the democracy to come with a suspension of the democracy that has been. In the movement between Europe and Africa, a Mediterranean thinking of movement and differentiation between continents, memories, and peoples, time is infused with space and tries to wrest free of that materiality (the atavism of the uprooted), while at the same time space is infused with time and tries to twist away from the weight and allure of the past lost (spectral memory haunts every diaspora). The uprooted African that Derrida *is* maps this transcendental on to the empirical, existential geography of what he calls, in *Monolingualism of the Other*, the Judeo-Franco-Maghrebian identity, which then becomes, in the early pages of that book, simply the Franco-Maghrebian. Geography is history and memory. Geography is also place, displace, and re-place, something akin to what Deleuze and Guattari describe as the movement between deterritorialization and reterritorialization. Geography, in this sense, is structured as the zig-zag characteristic of all those early Derridean motifs: sign and signification, voice and writing, presence and absence, and so on. Derrida links no small bit of this conception of his own Africanness to the process of decolonization. Monolingualism, he notes at the close of *Monolingualism of the Other*, "has the threatening face and features of colonial hegemony," not because the monolingual is a cloak of colonial politics, but because of "what remains insurmountable in it . . . quite simply [that] the 'there is language,' a there is language which does not exist,' namely that there is no metalanguage."[4] *There is language* insofar as language travels, insofar as language moves across borders and, in that movement and its ability to move populations—language is not only psychic or material displacement, but also the displacement of peoples—language functions as a colonizing force. To be uprooted as the African he *is*, Derrida is the site, even incarnation, of this colonizing force, both as the uprooted African he *is* (deterritorialized) and as the hegemonic Judeo-Franco in the fractured and fracturing identity of the Judeo-Franco-Maghrebian (territorializing). The performative, the making *of*, the utterance that installs—or even just indicates what was already—the Other inside the Same.

A Brief Excursus into Emmanuel Levinas' Thought

Interestingly, especially in his later work on immigration, lingualisms, and cosmopolitanism, Derrida has put Levinas' work into what we could call, evoking Edward Said's famous essay, traveling practice. (Or, perhaps, Derrida's identification with Africa and his Algerian roots should indicate, from the beginning, that his reading of Levinas already moves the theory across various borders.) One could argue that Derrida's later work, with its active seeking out of the strange and the stranger *beyond* the borders of the familiar, is more Levinasian than Levinas' own reflections on the crossing of ethics and politics. In particular, I am thinking of how Derrida's reflections on monolingualism point to a key item transformed by moving the Levinasian theory of the other, the force of disruption and displacement: language itself. Levinas' conception of language is complex, but fundamentally modeled on continuity. Language remains the same, even as it becomes fractured and broken apart—is not every fracture a splitting of what is assumed to be single and identical? Continuity is therefore a (if not *the*) source-point of the problem. Derrida's early criticism of Levinas in "Violence and Metaphysics" makes this clear: speaking and writing moves the singular into the general, placing the enigma of the other into the economy of intersubjective meaning. This is the ethical import of Levinas' epistemological critique of Husserl, which Derrida turns back on Levinas with a recurrence of the Husserlian analysis. Intersubjectivity, because it proceeds from a sense of a shared world *first* (Husserl's concern was always with the possibility of science and scientificity), does not conceive alterity *radically*. Levinas' first task is to uproot the idea of the other, extract from the soil of intersubjectivity (nation, region, race, culture, politics), and thereby relocate the notion of the other in the non-ground of interruption, disturbance, and the complex temporality in which ethical experience "happens." Language is therefore the curling back of the Same, threatening philosophy's attempt to articulate alterity from within the terms of articulation itself. Derrida's "Violence and Metaphysics" saw this so well. So, in his later work, Levinas responds by recasting the subject and language as address, accusation, and the diachronic structure of the encounter. *That* notion of language cannot swallow up the other, but is, in a sense, swallowed up *by* the other. De-nucleated and carved out. Subjectivity itself trumps language from the (non-)position of the other who never appears in language, yet puts me under the accusative in the encounter I cannot recall. This is Levinas at his most radical and, let us be honest, his most incomprehensible. As it should be. Responsibility in the Levinasian sense never quite makes sense. How can responsibility to this language, speaking and response as disruption and displacement, speak to the uprooting of Derrida's Africanness?

There is a double moment here that deserves consideration, one that Derrida's later work picks up in such interesting detail. On the one hand, language cannot remain stable and is destabilized from the first utterance of an address. In this sense, language is never monolingual. No sameness of meaning can gather and neutralize difference. Language, like subjectivity and even, indeed, *in* subjectivity, de-nucleates (to use the Levinasian term here). On the other hand, the language of address, the way language speaks to me and how the alterity in it speaks against language, is always from one and the same place, which Levinas enigmatically names a *non*-place. But here there is a key difference, one that underscores the materiality of the Derridean diasporic thought, across the Mediterranean. For Levinas, for example, the non-place does not come from the world, so cannot be called a place proper; there is nothing worldly about the Levinasian Other and the disrupting power it holds. Difference and *différance*, on this account, never bears markers of cultural or historical difference. This means that the ethical address—and any politics of hospitality that might carry across—might *seem* to take place in its own kind of neutral zone. Again, Levinas describes in great detail how the face expresses and undoes its own expression and my encounter with that expression in the mode of *nudity*. Levinas goes so far as to say: we would never notice the Other's eye color in the address. The double movement here is between a kind of anti- or ante-monolingualism that nonetheless repeats a perhaps sublated version of the same. *Monolingualism in the very same moment monolingualism might be said to be surmounted.* The stakes are high in this moment. Indeed, in this context, we can register a new challenge to Levinas in Derrida's reflections on monolingualism and relations of domination. Derrida writes:

> Every monolingualism and monologism restores mastery or magistrality. It is by treating each language differently, by grafting languages onto one another, by playing on the multiplicity of languages and on the multiplicity of codes within every linguistic corpus that we can struggle at once against colonization in general, against the colonizing principle in general (and you know that it exerts itself well beyond the zones said to be subjected to colonization), against the domination of language or domination by language. The underlying hypothesis of this statement is that the unity of language is always a vested and manipulated simulacrum.[5]

There is much that warrants comment in this passage, and it is of particular note that Derrida locates monolingualism in both colonization and what he calls the colonizing principle. By widening the claim of monolingualism, and so also the meaning of colonialism beyond particular zones of domination *elsewhere*, Derrida returns the question to *us*. What sort of vested and manipulated simulacrum could be at work in the Levinasian prerogative, and so, by extension, so much of philosophy? And what is at stake in thinking outside that monolingual habit? Here, the question of monolingualism lies in two sites. One, the quiet universality of even the pretension to a radical thought of difference—for example, Levinas' thinking the ethical, subjectivity, time, and so on *as such*—and, two, the insistence on the neutrality of what troubles the orderly life of consciousness. If those senses of radical alterity claim to bear no markers from the world, and are therefore vacated of any historical experience whatsoever, then we are warranted in considering the presence of certain colonizing principles in even the language of disruption—and so also some first terms of decolonzing the complications of deconstruction.

We might consider, for example, the case of Édouard Glissant, the Martiniquan poet, novelist, and theorist (and someone in whose company Derrida has also addressed the problem of monolingualism). Glissant places the problem of alterity at the heart of his notion of a Caribbean poetics. Alterity registers in Glissant's work in a number of different tones, beginning with what he has called, on a number of occasions, the *right to opacity*. Cultural difference means, as a point of beginning, the right to opaque formulations and linguistic foundations, which in turn makes difference make a difference. Opacity seals difference as irreducible, rather than as variation on what is, ultimately, one and the same core of meaning and significance. Alterity also lies at the heart of what Glissant calls the open imaginary. Thinking must open itself, be opened by, and open up in the Other a sense of Otherness. Not in the interest of synthesis, of course, for difference is irreducible. In the interest of contact and chaotic transformation—what Glissant calls, in his signature term, *creolization*—opacity is put to work as the doubling of relation: protective of self (resistant to senses of totalization), yet also transformed by and transformative of all that is put in contact (open to transcendence). Indeed, both have to be thought at once, crossed and paradoxical. Lastly, alterity, in this context, is *global* and *globalizing*. Creolization is a process of global and transnational contact. This process of contact is already at the origins of the Caribbean as a cultural site—composed as it is out of the fragments of Atlantic cultural forms—as well as the reality of cultural formation in late- and post-modernity. We are already global. The Other shows up in that global moment, questioning us, yes, but also provoking the new. Glissant's work, not unlike Derrida's reflection on the monolingual, takes us from the thought of the other to the other of thought. That is, not an other who is the object of my thinking, but, instead an other who relocates and is relocated—there is always relation—to the threshold of thinking and creating. At this threshold lies not just a healthy sense of limits (something the world actually needs) but also new, emerging, and ultimately unexpected forms of political and cultural transformation of the imagination. *Another world is possible as another kind of already deconstructed space, time, and place.* But that world, for Glissant, is always worldly and informed by a multiplicity of historical experiences.

The Franco-Maghrebian interchange of the uprooted African Derrida *is* might be located just inside that multiplicity. Derrida is in complex space here, for sure. Each moment wants to twist free and break. The spatialization of *life* in Africa, then in France, draws the thinker into that place; Derrida concedes again and again to being "a European intellectual." But at the same time, every diaspora has spectral memory; the dream and memory of what came before, the Algeria between colonized and before colonizing, draws thinking out of that space into the temporality of memory and history. And then back again to the spatiality of the thinker, incarnate and speaking, speaking his own incarnation into, then out of, being—a zig-zag movement between origin and form and formulation. This is perhaps Derrida's earliest thought, one that structures his

Introduction to Husserl's *Origin of Geometry*. It is also the thought of deconstruction in and as diaspora. A Mediterranean thinking between continents, drowning distinction but also roots in every passage.

CINDERAFRICA

The chiasmic relation of deconstruction and diaspora, if that is the relation they have, is about sites. Two sites, in fact, but like the fate of all things numerological in Derrida's work, the two mix and multiply. At the same time, Derrida's later work, especially *Monolingualism of the Other*, is often infused with the vicissitudes of nostalgia, longing, and critique. That infusion is about the possibility of another (deconstructed, diasporic) world, a kind of cosmopolitanism of identity and meaning that at once theorizes the boundary or border (the African, the I, the *am*) and pushes that theorized line to its vanishing point in time, absorbed, then expelled, by movement, memory, and specters (the uprooted, the I who recurs rather than persists, the *am* that is claimed by zig-zagging time).

This possibility of another world, site as diaspora, turns the question back to a second register of this enigmatic phrase "the uprooted African that I am." While the first register is one of a twisting and a turning that does not break free, but instead bears the transformative debt of the supplement and describes the hobbled dispersal of thinking diaspora, a second register returns to the sense of loss in the moment of uprooting and staggers any sense of an atavistic identity. Roots give life. Uprooting risks life. Indeed, even when life returns in the re-rooting of the uprooted roots, it draws from different wells, different earth, different *space* while being also constituted by the remainder of the past, the flesh of what has been, that time of the other which is also the time of the same. That is the complexity of the uproot*ing* of the uproot*ed*. Each partakes of life, but is also constituted by a certain death. Recall the logic of that great Presocratic dust up between Heraclitus and Parmenides, something they share even as they split the Occident's metaphysical tradition: loss and movement are inseparable. You cannot have one without the other. As well, there is the sense of loss inscribed within the deconstructive conjugation that declares the infusion of the subject with being and Being. There can never be a pure declaration of being or Being; from the earliest, Derrida insisted on the loss inherent in every declaration (writing is a tomb even as it gives life to possibility), not just as a spreading out or dispersal— though that is plenty—but as a disconnection that *defers*. The deferring moment of *différance* is a fracturing of identity, which means, and this is always such a difficult insight to bear from Derrida's early work, every life is a form of death, every identity is a form of loss, life in death. An identity that is asserted in the wake of the disruptive and displacing work uprooting doubles death and loss. The hyphen of the Franco-Maghrebian, and even the second hyphen of the occasional Judeo-Franco-Maghrebian, is a marker of loss that gives life, a life that gives loss. Dispersal is a doubling that calls for mourning. How do we make sense of this doubling?

Deferral and loss hearken back, for me, to one of Derrida's largely forgotten works, the 1982 essay, then 1987 book-length expansion, on the theme of loss and its figure: *Cinders*. In this long essay, which is partly a reflection on the moment of reflection on the figure of the cinder, but also an at times oblique meditation on the Shoah, Derrida mixes the cinder with mourning and the cenotaph. The argument, such as it is, wants to seal or entomb the memory of loss in order to forestall the colonization of memory by the metaphysics of presence. In a certain sense, this is Derrida rewriting Nicolas Abraham and Mária Török's meditation on introjection. The interest there is important, because it establishes the psychoanalytic traffic of the text, but even that traffic and the interest that produces it are drawn from his earliest reflections on the non-teleological structure of deferral. Without purpose or end, deferral structures the living present. Deconstruction wanders every text into that living present, into the space and time of deferral, just as the movement of diaspora defers belonging and suspends it between past and present.

In *Cinders*, this is formalized as the cenotaph. If the cenotaph is the memorial marker—a note in space, a stamp on the flow of time—that is not attached to that which is remembered, then the empty tomb figures precisely the memory of loss and what it does and does not, can and cannot, carry into the present. Language gives memory to the present. But the word is fragile. Monolingualism *chooses* time, fixing Derrida in the single-ness of language, and thereby carries only particular times and spaces of memory, or perhaps loses memory altogether. Or at least that is the challenge of the monolingual, to dwell in that single-ness without the violence of the Same precisely because the time of the Same is always an intervention and insertion into the time of the Other. *Cinders* dramatizes the death in intervention, the doubled silence of the Other in the Same. Derrida writes:

> But the urn of language is so fragile. It crumbles and immediately you blow into the dust of words which are the cinder itself . . . [T]his is not the tomb he would have dreamed of in order that there may be a place, as they say, for the work of mourning to take its time. In this sentence, I see the tomb of a tomb, the monument of an impossible tomb—forbidden, like the memory of a cenotaph, deprived of the patience of mourning, denied also the slow decomposition that shelters, locates, lodges, hospitalizes itself in you while you eat the pieces . . . An incineration celebrates perhaps the nothing of the all, its destruction without return but mad with its desire and with its cunning . . . [6]

Derrida here moves from loss to survival, from the remains to the remainder and its afterlife-of-sorts. Every life is a kind of death, every death is a kind of life; there really cannot be a distinction at this point. This is from the beginning the fundamental meaning of deconstruction. An impossible tomb doubles down on that claim about life and death, however; even death is structured by its own dying. Mourning would hold what is lost close to the act and action of mourning's memory, and that holding would compromise the death of death. The cinder pushes the idea of uprooting so far, perhaps further than Derrida is ready to bear in his own thought of the uprooted African he *is*. The uprooted as cinder would set memory afloat in the Mediterranean, then watch it drown, and then arrive and wonder what has been and what will be—the arrival that constitutes a diaspora as diaspora. From arrival to wondering, then, there is the stretch of crucial time and the decomposition of time, the cindering of time, the afloat that drowns and then the dragging ashore to start new. What if the hyphen cancelled more than it joined? *Cinders* is a radical text.

While this tearing apart and fiery decomposition that is the cinder underscores the loss inherent in transition, dispersal, and uprooting—the constitutive elements of diaspora—it is also a mixing of metaphors. The cinder burns, leaves ashes that blow away or are swept away, and whatever glows can only glow because of the profundity of irretrievable loss. This is the figure of the Shoah. The ashen memory that drove Nelly Sachs insane, the smokestack that did the same to Paul Celan. It is, after 1945, the constitutive loss of the Jewish diaspora. But the uprooting of the African Derrida *is* is a watery thought, a sort of anti-fire that also makes for unspeakable loss. The Mediterranean drowns memory, now by the thousands, as did the Atlantic for many centuries before it. Derrida's uprooting, marked by the hyphenation of Franco-Maghrebian quasi-identity, crosses the ocean, and so is no cinder. It does not burn. It does not leave ashes. And yet, there it is: this is the doubling of loss in the uprooted *Jewish* African Derrida *is*. To be ashen and drown at the same time, to be constituted by those two forms of loss and live within the remainder of both, while at the same time having to or wanting to say yes to life because every death is also life. This is no dialectic, of course. Derrida's zig-zag movement puts loss at the heart of diaspora and deconstruction—let us place them together here—in order for there to be life, and it is only because there is life that there is death. Derek Walcott claimed the sea as history, the ocean bottom as an archaeological site of diasporic becoming-life in the Americas. Derrida's sea is not history. It is cinder and cenotaph, somehow, in that odd place we call deconstruction, there is fire and ash at the bottom of the Mediterranean. He cannot *be* as uprooted except for that fire and ash at the bottom of the Mediterranean. This reminds us that deconstruction is often done with tears. Are you a person of the book, Professor Derrida? Or are you a person of the sea? Perhaps you are both and we have to reckon with that.

DWELLAFRICA

What comes after loss, especially when loss clings to the present (space) and spectral memory (time) in the place and non-place of dispersal? That is, what comes of the uprooted?

I am putting these questions to Derrida's texts, of course, and drawing long on the joint of one snippet of an utterance. But I think this is also the trajectory of his own thinking. To be sure, there is a kind of obsessive return to the death-effect of deconstruction in, say, *Of Grammatology* or the playfulness of *The Postcard*, not to mention all of those meta-reflections on knowing, speaking, and being in the earliest work, especially the Introduction to Husserl's *Origin of Geometry*, *Voice and Phenomenon*, and many of the essays collected in *Writing and Difference*. This sometimes meant the death of a particular concept—the sign, the voice, graphic inscription—and this sometimes meant the death of a philosopher's dream—Husserl's sad aspiration for origin(s) or monological foundation in the voice speaking to itself, quiet distinctions in Heidegger's footnotes, or the purity of Levinasian thinking. But later, I think it is fair to say that Derrida begins to wonder more boldly and more urgently about what comes *after* the death-effect of deconstruction. This is nothing like a retreat from the radical thought of deconstruction; indeed, if every death is a form of life and every life is a form of death, the question of what comes after *must* be a Derridean question. And so we have the problem of autoimmunity, which kills off or suspends (forms of death) in order to keep alive or sustain something that is riddled with finitude and vulnerability (democracy, Europe, the Other). Language is always the caveat here, for there is only one language, as Derrida says repeatedly in *Monolingualism of the Other*, and yet we are called for more, called to the non-monolingualism of the encounter, whether that is the encounter with the globalized and globalizing other or simply, perhaps more complexly (it is impossible to know), the encounter with oneself as the other of itself, split yet constituted by the dispersal of the diasporic subject.

And so, now, a third register of "the uprooted African that I am," one that sets the claim in the context of monolingualism. The uprooting of Derrida the African is a form of violence, and the difficulty of that violence is borne by the identity-as-being claim: he *is* African. That is the Maghrebian in the hyphenated name for Jacques Derrida. And yet he speaks French, which means the word works in and against the geography of the Maghreb and its spectral memory. This returns us to the earliest of Derridean motifs: in so many ways, violence takes the form of enactment in and as language. To speak and to write *after* displacement and dispersal—to speak in the diaspora—is to bear witness to, perhaps even reproduce, the violence of being uprooted. That is, to *become* the hyphen of the Franco-Maghrebian is to speak French, and so to bear witness to the colonizing force of monolingual.

This colonizing force, against which Derrida can only gesture types of resistance, wondering again and again what struggle there is to wage against it all, is what blocks the purity of any understanding of his claim to (uprooted) Africanness. There can be no exposition of the self. Loss, we should recall, is constitutive of the hyphen, even if the hyphen also bears life within and across it. Derrida writes in the Epilogue to *Monolingualism of the Other*:

> What I am sketching here is, above all, not the beginning of some autobiographical or anamnestic outline, nor even a timid essay toward an intellectual bildungsroman. Rather than an exposition of myself, it is an account of what will have placed an obstacle in the way of this auto-exposition for me.[7]

The experience of loss, and the failure to reassemble the fragments of Judaism, Europeanness, and the Maghreb and to seal up or purify *another world* or at least *another way of being* renders autobiography impossible. Derrida turns to monolingualism because monolingualism turns to, then against, him. Or, perhaps better, because monolingualism is *life* and is *what persists* after dispersal and loss, the element of life, language, is also the trafficking in death and the entombment of loss. Our lingualism is where we live; Heidegger was not wrong when he said language is the house of Being, he just did not understand it as a condition of profound violence and memory of loss. (Heidegger is no thinker of diaspora, to put it lightly.) Monolingualism, Derrida makes clear, is dwelling. And dwelling after loss, uprooting, and the vicissitudes of meaning that follow from that means dwelling in a language that *decides* (your speak yourself into being in French) what is fundamentally *undecidable* (the Franco-Maghrebian is not French, but also not Maghrebian). The hyphen is hope, I think, a hope that the "Franco" does not cancel or colonize or outright disappear the Maghreb, that there can be dual life, polylingualism, two forms of dwelling. So, while diaspora shatters and dis-assembles, monolingualism functions to both seal that shattering and calcify possibilities of thinking. The trace cannot make its way into language, even as the trace makes language possible; we know this from his earliest work. But in this moment, the trace is spectral memory and monolingualism is imperial space that makes its claim on the time of memory. Soon we will all forget whence we came. It might take generations, but there is forgetting. Not because humans are weak or lazy or tell underwhelming stories about the past (though all of those things are probably true), but because monolingualism is imperial. It is a space that conquers time. There is a cinder. It's all the diaspora has. It is very little, but not nothing.

What does it mean, then, to link monolingualism with dwelling? That is, what does it mean to set life inside of violence and the colonial, even as Derrida's own self-description struggles for the split and the hyphen, the anti-colonial? This is the question that begins *Monolingualism of the Other*, when Derrida writes:

> I am monolingual. My monolingualism dwells, and I call it my dwelling; it feels like one to me, and I remain in it and inhabit it. It inhabits me. The monolingualism in which I draw my very breath is, for me, my element. Not a natural element, not the transparency of the ether, but an absolute habitat. It is impassable, *indisputable*: I cannot challenge it except by testifying to its omnipresence in me. It would always have preceded me. It is me. For me, this monolingualism is me.[8]

What follows in the text, the body of what is obliquely indicated here as the constitutive and determining horizon of the monolingual, is what one expects from a Derridean text. A proclamation is set out—monolingualism is a form, if not *the* form, of dwelling—and then destabilized to a point at which one *might* think a non- or post-monolingualism would be possible, but then that possibility is retracted in the zig-zag movement of deconstructed meaning. And so Derrida in *Monolingualism of the Other* returns to dwelling, to the autobiographical, in order to underscore the simultaneous impossibility *and* the necessity of making words and stories and identities—the impossibility and necessity of the *is* in the uprooted African that Derrida *is*—even as they are consigned to death, which is also life, but, let's be real, is just so much death.

Diaspora is a painful discourse for this very reason. It is too often forced displacement and migration, and the hyphen does not speak to much life or living memory. Instead, there is deconstructive space and time, the space of uprootedness and the time of the ghost, that gives life with a measure of death. At the same time, there is speaking. And one might just have to find ways to make friends with, to say yes to, the ghost. In the monolingual, we catch sight of the necessity of autoimmunity—an impure struggle that kills in order to live. What is killed in the uprooting of Africa in order that Derrida might live as a European intellectual? And what is killed in the European intellectual in order that Derrida might write without the cinder, without the spectral memory, and instead from remainders of space *and* time from Africa? That is: what is Africa to Derrida? As deconstructive space, Africa is diaspora to Derrida. Suffering the violence of monolingualism, to be sure, but also its own agent of autoimmunity and the life that death gives. For all the force of the monolingual, Derrida will not cease to remind us that "the unity of language is always a vested and manipulated simulacrum."

In the end, Derrida's work bears out nicely the claim that deconstruction is fundamentally a diasporic thinking. This diasporic thinking is written into the general economy of language as the complex exchange/non-exchange of speech and writing, which is, in a certain sense, the relationship of roots and diasporic facticity. One finds one's self thrown—both as the ipseity of the I *here* in this place of displacedness and as the community, the we *here* in this place, of those without roots, a shared historicity of fractured historicality—into diasporic places. Thrownness itself, if I can re-import Heidegger's early concept of Dasein's fundamental condition, is already the loss of purity and the cancellation of the draw of origin. And yet origin echoes, speaks the subject back to a place *even when that place is unable to speak to or with or through the subject*. Derrida advances on the later Heidegger in precisely this sense: the Greek temple, as with the Presocratic word(s) more generally, fails, not because we have forgotten the sounding of Being in the word, but because Heidegger, unlike Derrida, has not theorized the deconstructive anti-structure of subjectivity—the uprooted Greek that you are, Martin Heidegger.

And yet, it is critical to note and sit with the fact that Derrida marks Africanness and uprootedness, that deconstructive double that makes a single subject, with being. *I am*. Therein lies the significance of all of this for thinking diaspora. It is a hyphen game. And the hyphen is all about the various paths of life and death. Life is preserved in the undecidable. Death deals from the coloniality of decision.

At the same time, it is worth asking about the monolingualism Derrida *is*, which is really just the uprootedness of the uprooted African that he is. I wonder, and this is my closing question, if there isn't something underdeveloped in this moment, something that is particularly linked to the Mediterranean passage specific to Derrida's becoming, after the uprooting, and European intellectual. What we do *not* find in this moment of displacement is one of the characteristic features of black diasporic life in the Americas: vernacular cultural forms. In particular, I am thinking of Glissant's long reflections on creole language and creolized cultural forms, something pushed even further by his self-proclaimed "children" Jean Bernabé, Patrick Chamoiseau, and Raphael Confiant. Creolization and vernacularity both name ways in which the hyphen is a condition, yes, of loss and death, but also a site of contestation of colonialism through the mixture of each side of the hyphen—always multiple and multiplying—with the other and Other. That mixture puts death into the monolingual, which, at the very least, sets the monolingual into the dynamic of becoming. Glissant's Deleuzean move here is crucial. He does not juxtapose creolization and monolingualism in terms of a polylingualism. Such a juxtaposition would reproduce the calcifications against which creolization struggles. Instead, there is, for Glissant, the rhizomatic knowing and being of creole language, alive and without dictionary, resistant to index and translation, composed of all the vernacular forms that come from the *djobber*—an odd-job worker with many skills, adapted to the moment, but servant to no one. Is there space for deconstructive thinking in this becoming-creole, in this anarchic vernacular mixture and contamination?

What if, then, we were to re-uproot the African Derrida *is*, and ask, with our own power as readers, what an African Derrida would look like, not as an African intellectual, but, in the becoming-space of diaspora, as a vernacular intellectual suspended in and making language from—not after—the hyphen which he *is* and imagines himself to *be*?

NOTES

1. Jacques Derrida, "The Crisis in the Teaching of Philosophy" in *Who's Afraid of Philosophy: Right to Philosophy I*, trs. Jan Plug (Stanford: Stanford University Press, 2002), p.103.
2. Jacques Derrida, "The Crisis in the Teaching of Philosophy" in *Who's Afraid of Philosophy: Right to Philosophy I*, trs. Jan Plug (Stanford: Stanford University Press, 2002), p.103.
3. Jacques Derrida, "*Différance*," in *Margins of Philosophy*, trs. Alan Bass (Chicago: University of Chicago Press, 1984), 8.
4. Jacques Derrida, *Monolingualism of the Other, Or, The Prosthesis of Origin*, trs. Patrick Mensah (Palo Alto: Stanford University Press, 1998), 69.
5. Jacques Derrida, *Who's Afraid of Philosophy: Right to Philosophy I*, trs. Jan Plug (Stanford: Stanford University Press, 2002), p.105.
6. Jacques Derrida, *Cinders*, trs. Ned Lukacher (Chicago: University of Chicago Press, 1991), 53/55.
7. Jacques Derrida, *Monolingualism of the Other, Or, The Prosthesis of Origin*, trs. Patrick Mensah (Palo Alto: Stanford University Press, 1998), 1.
8. Ibid.

WORKS CITED

Jacques Derrida, *Cinders*, trs. Ned Lukacher (Chicago: University of Chicago Press, 1991).

———, "*Différance*," in *Margins of Philosophy*, trs. Alan Bass (Chicago: University of Chicago Press, 1984).

———, *Monolingualism of the Other, Or, The Prosthesis of Origin*, trs. Patrick Mensah (Palo Alto: Stanford University Press, 1998).

———, *Who's Afraid of Philosophy: Right to Philosophy I*, trs. Jan Plug (Stanford: Stanford University Press, 2002).

THREE

Jacques Derrida

Figure of Maternal Thought

Nicolette Bragg

These days, the emancipatory ambitions of theoretical thought seem to generate only fatigue. This fatigue is inevitable, perhaps, as theory can be consuming. Concerned as it is with the constraining conditions of a personal experience of the world, critical theory draws the very self into its considerations of subjugation. Raymond Williams's definition of hegemony is telling in this regard. Describing a "whole body of practices and expectations, over the whole of our living," Williams identifies a reason for theory's encompassing habit of suspicion: hegemony "constitutes a sense of reality for most people in the society, a sense of absolute because experienced reality beyond which it is very difficult for most members of the society to move, in most areas of their lives."[1] The emancipatory goal of theory is not only to point out or to remedy social injustice; its style of thought responds to the self's inextricability from its own formation. Its focus is a "sense of reality," a subject of such intimacy that it is difficult to distinguish it from its own critique.

For many, fatigue results also from the way habits or styles of thought have come to replace a sustained consideration of specific and complex concerns. For example, although Eve Sedgwick recognizes that critique usefully reveals and responds to ideology and to the implications of socially produced meaning, she nevertheless associates it with a sense of suffocation: "it is possible that the very productive critical habits embodied in what Paul Ricoeur memorably called "the hermeneutics of suspicion"—widespread critical habits indeed, perhaps by now nearly synonymous with criticism itself—may have had an unintentionally stultifying effect."[2] Similarly Bruno Latour argues that intellectual responses have become "mechanical" and fruitless: "What if explanations resorting automatically to power, society, discourse had outlived their usefulness and deteriorated to the point of now feeding the most gullible sort of critique?"[3] Rita Felski's *Limits of Critique* provides another example, calling critique a "repeated practice" that obscures other ways to respond to a text.[4]

The problem with these "habits" is that they can curtail emancipatory projects. Mari Ruti describes one of theory's "bad habits" as a tendency to refuse the possibility of subjectivity. Theory has the habit, she maintains, of "leap[ing] from the (warranted) critique of the autonomous and sovereign subject of humanist metaphysics to the (in my view absurd) notion that all efforts at subjective recentering should be discouraged."[5] Considering that theory emerges in response to hegemony and ideology, the destruction of the subject seems a logical goal: De-subjectivization is an act of liberation from subjugating discourses and norms, considered to be a condition of thinking and the emergence of a mode of knowledge that troubles held beliefs. Ruti's point, however, is that it is not feasible to live a life according to the lingering postmodern aesthetic of theory, with decisions determined by "fragmentation, disintegration, decentering, disunity, fluidity, mobility, and volatility."[6] The desire to undo the subject has become empty, neglecting the real precarity of subject positions by establishing refusal and uncertainty as ethical responses to subjugation.

To sum this up in very broad strokes, the argument against critical theory is that it undervalues or disavows the possibility of subjectivity, agency, or voice. This is concerning as subjectivity is often unguaranteed—it's something for which many have to strive—or it is marked by a precarity that calls for its affirmation and imagination, rather than its disavowal. Theory has become associated with what falls beyond or outside subjectivity, of how we fall apart, for example, or of how we never come together. The argument against theory's habits therefore makes sense. When confronted with despair or desperation, with struggles to achieve representation, with psychic distress or trauma, many would see subjecthood as something for which to care. Many do yearn, at times, for a reparative mode of thought, for a consideration of attachment and belonging, for forms of healing.

The question of Jacques Derrida as a figure of African thought throws this discontent with theory into even sharper relief, as it situates these habits in relation to decolonial thought. When Peter Hallward juxtaposes the specific thought of Franz Fanon with the singularity of postcolonial thought, he throws into relief the possible limitations of de-subjectivization. For Hallward, Fanon demonstrates the possibility of political will, something he argues postcolonial theory has relegated to the "dustbin of conceptual history".[7] He reminds that Fanon, after Sartre, would teach one "to hold oneself, like a sliver, to the heart of the world, to interrupt if necessary the rhythm of the world, to upset, if necessary, the chain of command, but in any case, and most assuredly, to stand up to the world."[8]

This image is striking. While theory offers a host of alternatives to this sliver—including ideas of becoming, pluralities, undoing, ruptures, cyborgs—all of which reveal the potential of imaginative practices of exceeding subjugation to survive, the potential of knowing and withstanding the world requires a bolder and more radical act of imagination. Fanon's image captures the possibility of imagining one's own formation of one's own boundaries, one's own sense of self, after their eradication or its undoing, a way of establishing for oneself what was taken away: the very possibility of self-generation. The clarity of the image provides relief from the indeterminacies of theory—its blurring of boundaries, its evasion of the possibility of identity, its contingency and interdependence—and hazards a belief in the possibility of self-generation, the capacity to overcome one's own subjugation through forms of invention.

Interested in the possibility of self-generation, this chapter charts an alternative reading of theory, focusing specifically on Derrida. Conventionally, Derrida is understood to complicate the value of self-generation. *Monolingualism of the Other*, for example, a text that engages with his upbringing in Algeria, the changing status of his French citizenship, and his mother's loss of language, seems to foreground the lingering limits of self-generation, tracing not an attempt to invent oneself, but what interrupts this self-creation. Indeed, if decolonization differently crystalizes the question of subjectivity, bringing attention to dispossession, attachment, and belonging, then Derrida appears to undo the potential of this crystallization and what it reminds us to consider. Does Derrida not trouble the possibility of self-generation, of self-formation as the end of struggle?

By attending to and extending the idea of "generation," this chapter argues that, rather than opposing self-generation or theorizing its limits and failures, Derrida attempts to articulate a space between self and generation, a space that lays bare the ways in which the possibility of resistance or of being able to stand up to the world depends on being able to yield to another. Through a reading of *Of Hospitality*, it raises the possibility that one's border and boundaries can only be recuperated by moving through the messy space of encounter and the different forms of yielding and estrangement it demands. Finally, it presents this attempt as a form of maternity. The figure of the mother, usually linked so clearly to identity, to belonging, to attachment, comes to elaborate this different mode of coming into being. It is a maternal thought. Rather than "becoming men," Derrida would "become mother."

THE QUESTION OF BIRTH

To understand the significance of a "maternal" approach to the question of self-generation, it is helpful to keep in mind the centrality of birth to theories of subjectivity. As even a cursory overview of theory would show, subjectivity is often presented in relation to one's own birth. Subjectivity is presented as a form of overcoming birth. This means that at the heart of many theories of subjectivity is a concern about one's own birth or about the implications of one's birth to one's own sense of self or sense of belonging. Subjectivity is always tethered to birth, or it is frustrated by birth, or it is made possible by birth. This idea that subjectivity is related to the overcoming of one's birth also influences representations of maternity. The mother comes to be thought in relation to one's own attitude to one's own birth. Turning to recent theory and, in particular, to Derrida's own work on the subject, this section considers how birth circumscribes the question of self-generation.

A few examples will demonstrate how subjectivity came to be viewed as the overcoming of birth. Judith Butler's recent work on precariousness provides one example. Developing her theorization of susceptibility in *Senses of the Subject*, Butler describes the common antipathy or concern the sovereign individual has toward his own birth. As she points out, this concern is evident in writers who struggle to get "around the difficulty of once having been an infant unable to speak, reflect, or think as an adult author does."[9] The desire to write highlights this problem: writing would "counter and displace the infant's passivity and the lack of motor control, a resistance perhaps to needing to be in the hands of those he never chose, who turned out to care for him more or less well."[10] This primary vulnerability is of immense concern to the autonomous self the adult considers himself to be: "I may wish to reconstitute my 'self' as if it were there all along, a tacit ego with acumen from the start."[11] In short, the fact that one was born is a source of anxiety, getting in the way of one's perceived self-control and self-possession.

The idea of birth as that which troubles the adult's idea of his own sovereignty is also central to Elissa Marder's *The Mother in the Age of Mechnical Reproduction*. Responding to different cultural texts that recall and repeat the apparently singular event of birth, Marder highlights both the centrality and the inaccessibility of this formative event:

> However much we might want to lay claim to having a unique relation to the singularity of the event of our own birth, we have no direct access to it. We remain both bound to and exiled from our own birth. As an event, birth accrues and produces psychic meanings long before there is anyone 'home' in the self who would be able to attempt to read those meanings. In this sense, the event of the birth is not our own, even if it is profoundly and uniquely addressed to us.[12]

The inaccessibility of birth is troubling as it hinders our sense of autonomy and ownership. Birth is an act that befell us before we were us, the thing we must know or must leave behind in order to occupy and to know the limit of our own lives.

The connection of self-invention to the overcoming of birth is also central to Derrida's discussion of matricidal writing. Derrida dwells on this tension in his preface to Jacques Trilling's *James Joyce ou l'écriture matricide*. Although the preface, "The Night Watch (over 'the book of himself')," responds to Trilling's argument that writing is inevitably matricidal—always trying to kill the mother—it ends up focusing on the degree to which one's own birth interrupts and prevents one's own sense of sovereignty. Temporarily suspending the question of matricide, Derrida argues that writing is driven by the desire to undo one's own birth. He calls writing "the suicidal illusion . . . of giving birth to oneself. On one's own, freely, to oneself. . . . Auto-parthenogenesis of a writing, for example, that would like to deny or—for this amounts to the same thing—to appropriate without remainder the entirety of one's heritage."[13]

In other words, Derrida highlights the idea that self-invention is a way to get over one's own birth. By describing writing as "Auto-parthenogenesis," Derrida joins various dreams of self-formation that are distinct from birth, thus aligning cultural and literal production as forms of self-invention that transcend and overcome birth. While he argues for the impossibility and the cruelty of this attempted transcendence, he nevertheless firmly underlines the connection between selfhood and the ideals of sovereignty and self-possession and the overcoming of one's own birth. This desire to undo birth derives from what it signifies: birth signifies contingency, conditionality, and dependence, birth links one to a date, to a proper name, to cutting, to inscription, to a series of impositions and certifications that simultaneously contextualize one and challenge the force of textualization. Birth designates the dependence of formation on another's act. As Michael Naas puts it in his response to "The Night Watch," birth is "the very givenness or ineluctability of the origin, the always-already-givenness of the mark."[14] To recall Butler, it is the thought of our own susceptibility, our lack of choice over who raises us. To recall Marder, it is that formative event to which we have no access, that signals the limit to our own self-knowledge, to the edge of our story.

In this way, Derrida responds to some of the concerns birth raises in relation in political thought, challenging maternity as a trope of belonging and determination. In particular, he responds to Sigmund Freud's claim in "Notes upon a Case of Obsessional Neurosis" that what is notable about the identity of the mother is her certainty:

> As Lichtenberg says, "An astronomer knows whether the moon is inhabited or not with about as much certainty as he knows who was his father, but not with so much certainty as he knows who was his moth-

er." . . . A great advance was made in civilization when men decided to put their inferences on a level with the testimony of their senses and to make the step from matriarchy to patriarchy.[15]

Beyond the problematic hierarchy it establishes between sense and inference, Freud's description haunts political appropriations of birth and maternity. This is what Derrida would undo. Calling Freud's claim one of "the most salient limits and credulities of a certain Freudian discourse. Indeed, of its patriarchal phallogocentrism," Derrida refutes the idea that the mother is immediately identifiable.[16] Returning to questions emerging from developments in reproductive technology that have long been of concern to feminist scholarship, "The Night Watch" argues that there is no such thing as a "real" mother and that the idea that one can identify one's mother has always been a fiction. The mother is "a sort of speculative object susceptible to substitution."[17] The mother—the idea of a "real" mother—is a spectral construction of identity that hides her plurality and in-determinability.

This argument is compelling. Derrida's argument against the naturalness and determinability of the mother mirrors those for construction over biology and for culture over nature. It thus intervenes in problematic theories of the intrinsic belonging between motherhood and femininity or sexuality. It also counters conventional thoughts that would politicize natality, belonging, and kinship, and that set the stage for xenophobic and purist nationalisms and territorializations. It also challenges notions of inheritance, which presumes the singularity and certainty of the mother. As Naas explains, all of these depend on an illusion of the "naturalness and purity of women [which is] even more resistant to interruption, questioning, or critique than the phallogocentric phantasm of the sovereign, engendering power of men."[18] In other words, in denying the mother's singularity, Derrida intervenes in political appropriations and ramifications of birth.

In addition to this, the argument enables provocative theorizations of the mother. On the one hand, Derrida's argument of the substitutable mother complements his assertion of the phantasmatic properties of identity—not only is the idea of a real mother complicit in the notion of a single origin or natural belonging, but the mother is an exemplar figure of singularity; her substitutability marks the exposure of the deeply unsettling fiction of a core belief. On the other hand, his argument presents the mother as an example of the instability within the very idea of identity. "Mother" becomes a discursively disruptive classification and identification, erroneously signifying the singular but generating the many. The mother's substitutability reacts with the illusion of her singularity, producing bewildering proliferations of the unique that cannot be accommodated within language. The identity, "mother," can be occupied by many, can refer to more than one, it is a category that is supposed to belong exclusively to one but that incorporates many and that belongs to many. She emerges as a figure for an impossible containment of plurality and instability: "Now the most difficult thing to think, and first of all desire, then to accept otherwise than as a monstrosity, is precisely this: more than one mother. Supplements of mothers, in an irreducible plurality..."[19]

Is this itself matricidal? In its attempt to let go of this figure of the real mother, could Derrida's writing itself be defined as "matricidal?" He would undo the figure of the mother, he would fictionalize the real, or realize the fiction, and he would substitute this figure of origin and belonging with the act of writing. In other words, it seems that Derrida's treatment of birth raises the troubling questions about identity and subjectivity that lead to discontent with theory, and that it does so without proposing the possibility of self-generation. He links the idea of a single, identifiable, unique mother to the phantasm of identity, and to its necessary and sustaining narratives of a single, locatable origin.

Yet, this is not the final word on birth. Although theory's representation of maternity seems to only problematize the desire for generation, there is another possible approach to this relation. For one, the meaning of "birth" is not fixed. "Birth" does not only refer to the event from the past that determines the future of an individual. For another, the meaning of "mother" is also not fixed. The "mother" can be thought beyond the relation to this birth of the past, this birth that can be imagined to be one's own. In his interviews with Elisabeth Roudinesco, Derrida gestures to the possibility of a new meaning: "But what is it to be born?" he asks. Questioning the limits of philosophical and psychoanalytic approaches to the subject, he suggests that

> If we can distinguish it rigorously from the origin, the beginning, provenance, etc., 'birth' is perhaps a question of the future and of arrival, a newly arrived question [*une question d'avenir, une question toute neuve*]. Philosophy is much more prepared to work on questions of the origin and the end, of life and death. But philosophy (and no doubt science too, most often, and in any case psychoanalysis) has given little 'thinking' attention to what, in birth, does not fall under these categories.[20]

As birth and maternity are central to the question of subjectivity, their meaning matters. Reconsidering this meaning shakes up the patterns of thought around the possibility and the perception of subjectivity, potentially allowing new visions of self-generation.

MATERNITY AS A NEW QUESTION OF ARRIVAL

In the postscript to "The Night Watch," Derrida confesses a desire to stop writing. He claims that he wants "from now on, no more writing, especially not writing, for writing dreams of sovereignty, writing is *cruel*, murderous, suicidal, parricidal, matricidal, infanticidal, fratricidal, homicidal, and so on. Crimes against humanity, even genocide, begin here, as do crimes against *generation* . . . "[21] Rather than writing, he will love birth: "from now on, before and without the death toward which, as I have written elsewhere, *I advance*—to begin finally to love life, namely birth. Mine among others—notice I am not saying *beginning* with mine" (emphasis in original).[22] Coming after his discussion of matricide and the fiction of the real mother, the confession is surprising. Derrida does not only wish not to write; he wishes to love the mother. Quitting writing "would be a matter of beginning to love love without writing, without words, without murder. It would be necessary to begin to learn to love the mother—and maternity, in short, if you prefer to give it this name."[23] Derrida appears in this postscript to write toward what would otherwise be left behind, toward that which we would overcome. Although ambivalent and ambiguous, it is a gesture—a tracing—of what could be called his maternity, an exposure to birth as a newly arrived question.

What if understanding Derrida depends on a maternity of thought, one that derives from the exposure to an arrival without name or belonging? This section describes this new maternity, re-framing Derrida's meditations on hospitality and considering its implications for how we think of Derrida's thought in relation to Africa. Framed by this maternity, hospitality's formulations of uncertainty and impossibility become the outline of another way to come into being. This outline undoes the opposition between theory and the thought of self-generation, lessening the contrast between Fanon's sliver and theory's fog. It articulates the way in which resistance derives from one's capacity to yield to another. This is a self that comes when one's borders break, from processes of yielding to another, from encounter and exposure. As a coming into being, it traces the formative function of indeterminacy, the way habits of thought attend to the other. Derrida's characteristic indeterminacy, in other words, the resemblance of this thought to the "bad habit" of de-subjectivization, is precisely, also, self-generation.

Derrida's discussion of birth helps bring this into view. In "Artifactualities," Derrida argues that birth is an event, disrupting the context out of which it emerges:

> At the birth of a child, the primal figure of the absolute arrivant, you can analyze the causalities, the genealogical, genetic, or symbolic premises, and all the wedding preparations you like. Supposing this analysis could ever be exhausted, you will never get rid of the element [*l'alèa*], this place of the taking-place, there will still be someone who speaks, someone irreplaceable, an absolute initiative, another origin of the world.[24]

In this passage, birth does not mark the beginning of the self, but the arrival of another. In effect, Derrida steps to the other side of birth, viewing it not as an event of one's past, but as an event of a future other. Birth is that which brings together, is the togetherness of, the event and the arrival of the other. Birth is not expected, anticipated, or planned. Birth is disruptive, transformative, singular; it reconfigures the context out of which it arise.

This idea of birth as an event provides a new way to think of the figure of the mother. Thinking of birth as an event suspends the question of identification and instead prioritizes an exposure. Indeed, "mother" comes to signal not certainty, but a form of exposure, the risk of an exposure, the possibility of the event. "Mother" signals a relation to something that does not belong, that occurs in close proximity, and that necessitates a change in the frame of encounter. Furthermore, thinking of birth in terms of an event locates the mother at a scene of temporal disruption. This is a new maternity, a new way to think of this relation, one that falls beyond the framework of procreation or reproduction, but one that nevertheless introduces a mode of care and of encounter. This new maternity creates a new shape or template for Derrida's thought, a new legibility for his poetics of arrival.

As I show, new maternity maps onto Derrida's theory of hospitality, revealing it to be the articulation of the complex ways in which coming into being can be hinged to the possibility of another. To be sure, it is difficult to think about hospitality in the context of colonialism. Hospitality is the act of welcoming a stranger into one's home, and colonialism puts the possibility of "home" into question, confusing and troubling the notions of guest, stranger, and invitation. Derrida's take on the subject of hospitality increases this difficulty. In *Of Hospitality*, Derrida challenges hospitality as a model for ethical behavior, arguing that it is limited and violent as it depends on a home, a master, and a system of recognition that will define and potentially exclude the guest: there is "No hospitality, in the classic sense, without sovereignty of oneself over one's home, but since there is also no hospitality without finitude, sovereignty can only be exercised by filtering, choosing, and thus by excluding and doing violence."[25]

He offers, instead, the idea of "unconventional hospitality," a radical ethics that entails opening one's home without question or hesitation. It would extend beyond the identifiable categories of guest and would require that one "say yes to who or what turns up . . . whether or not the new arrival is the citizen of another country, a human, animal, or divine creature, a living or dead thing, male or female."[26] To theorize unconditional hospitality in the colonial situation is highly risky. It is challenging to support a theory that advises one to "*Say yes*," to "*Say yes*" to everyone and everything that arrives.

Yet, while unconditional hospitality describes a radical, impossible, impractical ethics, it also captures and encapsulates the effects of coming into confrontation with a stranger, effects that take shape as new modes of knowledge. For example, unconditional hospitality requires that I "open up my home and that I give not only to the foreigner . . . but to the absolute, unknown, anonymous other, and that I *give place* to them . . . "[27] This opening displaces and estranges the host from his or her home. On the one hand, this appears to recall the discontent with theory, prioritizing what lies beyond subjectivity. It appears an impossible poetics, a radical ethics that cannot survive specific contextualization or pertain to the real conditions of existence. On the other hand, it addresses the way in which the step beyond oneself is precisely what allows resistance, precisely what allows one to stand up to the world. This is the maternal aspect to his theory, that aspect which cannot be traced within the framework of self-possession or agency.

New maternity makes visible the way in which a decision can take place through the making possible of another. In "Hostipitality," Derrida insists that it is not the host, but the arrival, that decides hospitality. Echoing Martin Heidegger's *Was Heisst Denken?*, he argues: "we do not yet know who or what will come, nor what is called hospitality and what is called in hospitality, knowing that hospitality, in the first place, is called [*ça s'appelle*] . . . "[28] It is not the host, but the arrival that calls forth hospitality. The arrival to some degree therefore brings about the openness it requires, upsetting the temporality of the conditions for arrival, setting the arrival up a process or a tension. It is a relational act that draws both arrival and host into the establishment of hospitality. In short, unconditional hospitality denotes the process of the decentralization of self from responsibility that confuses the source of identity and action. Dependent on the other, hospitality describes the process of de-centralization that leads to the decision. Maternity brings into view this possibility: de-centralization can be the condition of resistance, the condition of making a decision, the way we stand up to the world.

This new maternal frame for Derrida's thought transforms the radical impossibility of hospitality and its poetics of selflessness into an account of the way in which one's own sense of one's borders and one's own capacity to stand up to the world come from the arrival of another who tests those borders. Unconventional hospitality is the path of individuation that takes place as the by-product of the possibility of another, that outsources self-formation, a construction of an outline that results from the putting in place of that which surrounds it. Building specificity around oneself, directed to oneself by another, breaking this divide between undoing oneself and taking a position, it suggests that resistance can come about as a process of being taken over. It considers the possibility that individuation comes about through the possibility of another's estranging arrival.

This encounter is an alternative to and echo of the self-generation Fanon presents in *Black Skins, White Masks*. It describes the way in which one's arrival depends on one's letting come of the other. It describes the way in which we know our boundaries by the added interaction with another. It is another way to take place. It is as if the boundaries that were never respected—that called into question the very possibility of subjectivity—can only be given back through the encounter with another. It raises the possibility, not only, that Derrida's emphasis on absolute welcome derives in part from a sensitivity to how much some depend on the withdrawal of boundaries, but that one's own arrival depends first on all the making possible of the arrival of another. Maternity makes legible the space between one's arrival and the other's, the way the former often depends on the latter, as if generation were also a necessary and unguaranteed process of yielding to another, as if we could never arrive without this yielding. They belong together. The two happen interrelatedly. New maternity, then, is the hope of political will in the face of lost boundaries, the self as the by-product of the encounter with another that shatters self-perception through a reinstation of these borders. Awareness, consciousness, transcendence, resistance, seen as ends in themselves, are not only unguaranteed, but they could only emerge by way of theory's promises: the liminality and blurring to which we are all subject.

TO BE OF AFRICA

What if theory were a dream of birth? This is the figure of Derrida's thought. Derrida's habits of thought could be understood as the repeated desire to respond to another, to keep himself exposed and so to effect an arrival. Writing always for the other, always making space for the other, Derrida writes to be in the position of this mother. His is a maternal writing. Making space for the other by haunting himself, by refusing to foresee the future, by refusing the promise of sense. He attempts, in other words, a maternity through writing. He advances to birth, to love birth.

This maternity re-situates Derrida in relation to the specific, political context of Algeria and decolonial struggle. Derrida displaces the question of his own origin in favor of the question of the arrival of the other. While the risk of turning to the mother and to birth to figure a form of thinking is high, it enables a thought to come into view that moves beyond identity but not beyond care, that derives from yielding to another, and from being transgressed. It suggests an aspect to any relation to another that is linked to thinking; it suggests the way in which tending toward another, inclining toward another, giving up oneself for the other, can be the foundation for a form of thinking whose tendencies and implications would otherwise remain unrecognizable. Although Derrida denies the existence of a "real" mother, he writes toward maternity through his own resistance to resolution, through his desire to burden himself, through his desire to be burdened. This is his question after Algeria, after its colonization, a question of the postcolonial: how can I advance toward the arrival, speak for the arrival, in the place of the arrival?

NOTES

1. Raymond Williams, *Marxism and Literature* (Oxford: Oxford University Press, 1976), 110.
2. Eve Kosofsky Sedgwick and Adam Frank, *Touching Feeling: Affect, Pedagogy, Performativity* (Durham: Duke University Press, 2003), 124.
3. Bruno Latour, "Why Has Critique Run Out of Steam? From Matters of Fact to Matters of Concern," *Critical Inquiry* 30, no. 2 (2004): 225-230.
4. Rita Felski, *The Limits of Critique* (Chicago: Chicago University Press, 2015), 21.
5. Mari Ruti, "The Bad Habits of Critical Theory," *The Comparatist* 40, no. 1 (2016): 5-27.
6. Ruti, "Bad Habits," 8.
7. Peter Hallward, "Fanon and Political Will," *Cosmos and History* 7, no. 1 (2001): 104-127.
8. Franz Fanon, *Black Skin, White Masks*, trans. Charles Lam Markmann (London: Pluto Press, 2008), 57.
9. Judith Butler, *Senses of the Subject* (New York: Fordham University Press, 2015), 3
10. Butler, *Senses*, 4
11. Judith Butler, *Precarious Life: The Powers of Mourning and Violence* (New York: Verso, 2004), 27.
12. Elissa Marder, *The Mother in the Age of Mechanical Reproduction: Psychoanalysis, Photography, Deconstruction* (New York: Fordham University Press, 2012): 3.
13. Jacques Derrida, "The Night Watch," trans. Pascale-Anne Brault and Michael Naas, in *Derrida and Joyce: Texts and Contexts*, ed. Andrew Mitchell and Sam Slote (Albany: State University of New York Press, 2013), 102.
14. Michael Naas, "The Mother, of All the Phantasms," in *Derrida and Joyce: Texts and Contexts* (Albany: State University of New York Press, 2013), 178.
15. See Derrida, "The Night Watch," 107.
16. Derrida, "The Night Watch," 107.
17. Derrida, "The Night Watch," 99.
18. Naas, Michael, "The Mother, of All the Phantasms," 171.
19. Jacques Derrida and Elisabeth Roudinesco. *For What Tomorrow: A Dialogue*, trans. Jeff Fort (Stanford: Stanford University Press, 2004), 41.
20. Derrida, *For What Tomorrow*, 40.
21. Derrida, "The Night Watch," 102.
22. Derrida, "The Night Watch," 102.
23. Derrida, "The Night Watch," 102.
24. Jacques Derrida, "Artifactualities," in *Echographies of Television: Filmed Interviews*, trans. Jennifer Bajorek. (Cambridge: Polity Press, 2002), 21.
25. Jacques Derrida, *Of Hospitality*, trans. by Rachel Bowlby. (Stanford: Stanford University Press, 2000), 55.
26. Derrida, *Of Hospitality*, 77.
27. Derrida, *Of Hospitality*, 25.
28. Jacques Derrida, "Hospitality," trans. Barry Stocker with Forbes Morlock, *Angelaki* 5 no. 3 (2000): 3-18.

WORKS CITED

Butler, Judith. *Senses of the Subject*. New York: Fordham University Press, 2015.

Derrida, Jacques. *Monolingualism of the Other, Or The Prosthesis of Origin*. Translated by Patrick Mensah. Stanford: Stanford University Press, 1998.
———. *Of Hospitality*. Translated by Rachel Bowlby. Stanford: Stanford University Press, 2000.
———. "Artifactualities." *Echographies of Television: Filmed Interviews*. Translated by Jennifer Bajorek. Cambridge: Polity Press, 2002. Print.
———. "Hostipitality." Translated by Barry Stocker with Forbes Morlock. *Angelaki* 5, no. 3 2000, 3-18.https://doi.org/10.1080/09697250020034706
———. "The Night Watch." Translated by Pascale-Anne Brault and Michael Naas. *Derrida and Joyce: Texts and Contexts*. Ed Andrew J Mitchell and Sam Slote. Albany: State University of New York Press, 2013: 87-108. Print.
Derrida, Jacques., and Elisabeth Roudinesco. *For What Tomorrow: A Dialogue*. Translated by Jeff Fort. Stanford: Stanford University Press, 2004. Print.
Fanon, Frantz. *Black Skin, White Masks*. Translated by Richard Philcox. New York: Grove Press, 2008.
Felski, Rita. *The Limits of Critique*. Chicago: Chicago University Press, 2015.
Hallward, Peter, "Fanon and Political Will." *Cosmos and History: The Journal of Natural and Social History* 7, no. 1 (2011): 104–127. https://cosmosandhistory.org/index.php/journal/article/view/244/338
Latour, Bruno. "Why Has Critique Run Out of Steam?: From Matters of Fact to Matters of Concern." *Critical Inquiry* 30, no. 2 (Winter 2004): 225-248. DOI: 10.1086/421123
Marder, Elissa. *The Mother in the Age of Mechanical Reproduction: Psychoanalysis, Photography, Deconstruction*. New York: Fordham University Press, 2012. Print.
Naas, Michael. "The Mother, of all the Phantasms." In *Derrida and Joyce: Texts and Contexts*. Ed Andrew J Mitchell and Sam Slote. Albany: State University of New York Press, 2013: 163–182. Print.
Ruti, Mari. "The Bad Habits of Critical Theory." *The Comparatist*. 40, no, 1 (2016): 5–27. https://muse.jhu.edu/article/635920.
Sedgwick, Eve Kosofsky and Adam Frank. *Touching Feeling: Affect, Pedagogy, Performativity*. Durham: Duke University Press, 2003.
Williams, Raymond. *Marxism and Literature*. Oxford: Oxford University Press, 1976.

FOUR
Setting, an Example

Derrida's South Africa (and Ours)

Jan Steyn

Jacques Derrida: a figure of African thought? The idea is provocative, but not obvious. Mention "Africa" and one rarely thinks of "Jacques Derrida;" mention "Derrida" and "Africa" is hardly the first connotation. Nicholas Royle in his popular primer *Jacques Derrida* (2003) never mentions Africa.[1] Nor does Simon Glendinning's *Derrida: A Very Short Introduction* (2011).[2] Royle does bring up *Algeria* in his book's first two pages but only to deconstruct the idea of biographical origin; Glendinning follows suit in beginning his book by talking about Derrida's place of birth and then immediately putting into question "that kind of starting point."[3] In Geoffrey Bennington's "Derridabase," his part in the collaboration with Derrida, *Jacques Derrida*, over the course of 420 pages including bibliography and notes, the words "Africa" or "African" appear a collective total of five times, three times in the context of Hegel's concept of African fetishism and twice in the biographical notes at the end, while Derrida's own contribution, "Circumfession," never even mentions the continent. In the case of the latter text, however, Africa, or North Africa, is the unnamed regional origin that Derrida shares with Augustine of Hippo, whose *Confessions* he admires, reflects, and reflects upon in that text. Unlike the texts of many of his most celebrated explicators, in Derrida's own writing Algeria features importantly, whether explicitly or as an open secret, especially in those texts that Benoît Peeters in his biography of Derrida calls "Memoirs that are not Memoirs."[4] However, what interests me in this chapter is Derrida's reflection on and in the other end of Africa: South Africa, which cannot be fitted for the role of (prosthesis of) origin. South Africa is never more than an example for Derrida, and yet, in texts such as "Racism's Last Word,"[5] "Admiration of Nelson Mandela: Or, the Laws of Reflection," the dedication of *Specters of Marx*,[6] and "On Forgiveness,"[7] it figures time and again as exemplary, or as illustration of the exemplarity of the example. The familiar dialectic between the local and the global (or, as it's often cast, between the national and the international) has been particularly pertinent to thinking South Africa both during and after apartheid. But the relation between South Africa and the world that Derrida posits, of South Africa as example—as in-forming and in-formed by larger systems, values or processes, as instance but also as (good or bad) model, used to set, illustrate, contest, or deconstruct would-be universal laws or principles—has never been more salient than during the recent "hashtag wars" and "Fallism" debates in South Africa. Salient but ignored. Pertinent but forgotten.

"Sovereign is he who decides on the exception,"[8] yes, but what of he who decides on the example? The example is never given, never self-sufficient. In as far as the example is exemplary, it looks outward, beyond itself, toward a larger principle. Insofar as there is a greater principle, there is always the possibility of another, different example. The example is always selected, chosen, partial. In this way the example is arbitrary and yet not. So too with the model, or "role model"—those select few human beings we consider exemplary. Their exemplarity is accompanied by a preposition or a qualifying clause; they are exemplary *of* a phenomenon, exemplary *as* an ideal, exemplary *at* a role, at once supplement and paragon of the ability or attribute that they embody. It is the example's role to make manifest, visible, and concrete what is general and abstract. To speak of the example without giving examples is to trade in generalities and forgo the power of concreteness that is the example's domain. And yet, to give *an* example of the example would move us away from the heart of the matter to its skin, from essence to surface, as principles give way to particulars and details come to overshadow universals. This is the fate of examples, inexorable as (for example) death. Never more so than when setting the example also entails choosing an exemplary setting. When *setting* refers to place it means more than grouping a *set* of elements according to abstract principle, and it implies more than simply fixing something already extant into a new context or frame as with the setting of a jewel. Places are inexhaustible in their detail, history, and complexity. When a place is asked to stand for a dynamic or a form, the embodiment is richer, fuller, easier to grasp, and yet more complex than the thing it embodies. It is the example that adumbrates and insists on the rule. And the person who decides on the example, who elevates the particular to exemplary status, is also the one who shapes principle—often into unintended forms.

So let us begin with an example and a setting: a scene in Kirby Dick and Amy Ziering Kofman's documentary, *Derrida*, where Derrida gives a lecture at the University of the Western Cape (UWC) about forgiveness, which follows another scene where Derrida visits Nelson Mandela's cell on Robben Island. We see Derrida standing at a lectern, addressing a packed lecture theater, saying,

> More than once will we be faced with a preliminary question, which is the question: who or what? Does one forgive someone for a wrong committed or does one forgive someone something? Someone who, in whatever way, can never be totally confused with the wrongdoing or the moment of the past wrongdoing nor with the past injury. So, the question is, who or what? Do we forgive someone, or do we forgive someone something?[9]

The film cuts to the moderator inviting a final question from the audience and then to an audience member challenging Derrida to speak to his status as "a white Western male, speaking to a white audience."[10] Of course, Derrida's so-called white-ness and so-called Western-ness can both be questioned, or perhaps rather deconstructed, and, as the camera silently underlines, so can the questioner's assumptions about the audience's homogeneity. Nevertheless, the audience member, whom the film's published screenplay designates as a "student," continues her interrogation:

> Now you may have meant that pure forgiveness thing with a lot of irony, and maybe that is something that is really impossible—pure forgiveness being really impossible, but we sit here as potential objects of forgiveness. We are, all of us, you included, in a sense guilty. Now . . . don't you think it fills an ideological function speaking to us, telling us in a sense we should not repent, not ask for forgiveness, because then we "ruin" pure, unconditional forgiveness, while at the same time you are telling oppressed people they should forgive without expecting repentance?[11]

Derrida is graceful enough not to take the "student" to task for her misrepresentations of his position—both of the position from which he speaks and of the position that he takes in the argument—but instead gives a good-natured response about the importance of irony and a recapitulation of why he believes it is important to distinguish between forgiveness as an ethical act and reconciliation as a political end. The next scene takes place in a garden where Derrida gives a more thorough and forceful version of this argument, this time in French, wherein he is careful to emphasize that while he holds to the aporetic structure of forgiveness—that only the unforgivable can be forgiven and that consequently to forgive is to do the impossible—he nevertheless supports political programs of reconciliation; he keeps the practical project of political reconciliation distinct from the theoretical horizon of "pure forgiveness," refusing to conflate the two. Derrida speaks of forgiveness in general, as a theoretical structure, while the "student" is concerned with forgiveness in the here and now of her setting. The film's editing implies that Derrida's statement in the garden is a second response to the UWC student, a case of philosophical *l'esprit de l'escalier* in a Cape Town garden after the public lecture. But the screenplay gives location as "EXT. LAGUNA BEACH—CALIFORNIA—DAY."[12] For all we know, this scene could have been shot *before* Derrida's South African trip. It is only a response to the South African student's question in as far as we are able to imagine the scene as still (or pre-emptively) responsive to the student's frustration with (what she believes to be) Derrida's disregard of (what she believes to be) the singularity of her context, that is a response from afar, from another context entirely. Changing the setting matters. It promotes forgiveness as a general, abstract phenomenon, the embodiments and implications of which can be sampled and analyzed from many different locations; it belies the urgency and supposed incommensurability implied by the deictic force of the student's statements—*this* forgiveness, on *this* university campus.

Derrida's questioner at UWC is not the first South African student to be incensed by (what she perceived to be) Derrida's insufficient attention to her unique historical context, to the extent of embarrassingly misreading *his* context and *his* argument.[13] Nor, we will see, is she the last South African student to insist on the abject singularity of her context, resisting any generalizing move that would reduce this context to the role of simply one example of some putatively broader or more universal dynamic.

The self-proclaimed, de-colonizing international movement that goes under the hashtag #RhodesMustFall, which has one of its origins in the defacement of a statue of Cecil John Rhodes on the University of Cape Town campus in March of 2015, is in many ways anarchic, de-cephalous and poly-vocal, therefore resistant to easy definition or representation. But it would be fair to say its origins and goals find their nexus in university life: #RhodesMustFall holds seminars, publishes pieces of collective writing, organizes reading groups, questions canons, debates institutional structures and accountability, and proposes alternative forms of intellectual engagement which, while differing from the university as it already exists, are always proposed in relation to it. It has been my experience—and here I must acknowledge my slippage between archival and anecdotal modes of documenting #RhodesMustFall, of inducing general rules from the examples I observe—that discussions among members more often than not feature Frantz Fanon, the chapters in common being "Concerning Violence" and "Pitfalls of National Consciousness" in *Wretched of the Earth* and "The Fact of Blackness" in *Black Skin, White Masks*. These readings inspire a theory of revolutionary violence, a critique of the current post-apartheid government as neocolonial elite, and, in a popular reading, a theory of black pain that is phenomenologically

Setting, an Example 51

inaccessible to non-black subjects who are consequently ethically barred from pronouncing on it. Gone is the non-racialism of the ANC, or, in an academic context, the *deconstruction* of race as a category; this (disputed) version of Fanonian thinking returns us to the brute racial essentialism and race-based solidarity and action of an earlier time.[14] Still, however dominant, this is only one strand of thinking or reading in the #RhodesMustFall movement; let us not elevate sample to example. The movement has, in fact, composed a broader "official" reading list, which is stored on—and is regularly removed from—dropbox.com. This list contains a far more extensive constellation of intellectual sources including, along with Fanon, philosophers, statesmen, Black Consciousness thinkers, and critical theorists: from Alain Badiou and Slavoj Žižek to Chinua Achebe and Ngũgĩ wa Thiong'o; from Steve Biko and Robert Sobukwe to Julius Nyerere and Haile Selassie; from Antonio Gramsci and Vladimir Lenin to Georg Hegel and Karl Marx; from Marcus Garvey and C.L.R. James to Chris Hani and Govan Mbeki . . . It's a long and fascinating list. And Derrida doesn't make the cut.

This is, of course, understandable. A reading list is only valuable in as far as it is selective, which is to say in as far as it excludes. Derrida and deconstruction have, however unfairly, been accused, regularly and at length by a variety of authoritative (largely Marxist) critics of failing to espouse an activist politics.[15] From an Africanist perspective, as E.C. Eze and Bruce Janz point out in their obituary of Derrida,

> There is much in his work to resist: the deep commitment to social justice or what he himself called the "democracy to come;" the insistence on the "event"—the surprising, improvisational character of utterance and agency; and the exhortation to attention or active waiting—an exercise in philosophical vigilance capable of frustrating even the most fervent and well-intentioned activist.[16]

So it is no surprise that an activist movement, even one that takes the written word and written traditions (philosophical and black intellectual) as seriously as #RhodesMustFall undoubtedly does, would choose to forgo the infamous rigors of reading Derrida. Understandable, yes, but a mistake. It is a mistake because while the dedication of *Specters of Marx* to Chris Hani may feel ad hoc, tagged on at the last moment, of marginal importance to the text, it describes and illustrates precisely the de-centering, anti-Narcissistic position of an example relative to what it exemplifies in a broader setting, something which #RhodesMustFall needs to think about in order to account for their international origins and trajectory. Because to grapple with "On Forgiveness" is to grapple with the relationship between (local and historical) context and unconditional principles, a relationship that is not always clear in #RhodesMustFall's interventions. Because "Racism's Last Word" speaks to us with no less urgency in a post-apartheid age. And, above all, because "Admiration of Nelson Mandela" is even more pressing now that we are post-Mandela.

But first, what is #RhodesMustFall? In March of 2015, a student at the University of Cape Town (UCT), Chumani Maxwele, took a bucket of human feces from Khayelitsha and dumped it over a statue of Cecil John Rhodes. The statue overlooked Cape Town from its central perch on the UCT campus, right below the university's principle gathering place and the steps leading up to them, "Jameson Hall" and "Jameson Steps," respectively. This was an act, as was obvious from the start to supporters and detractors alike, for which contexts, settings, and proper names were highly significant. Khayelitsha township is a large hybrid formal/informal settlement bordering other vast shanty towns, working-class townships, and lower-middle-class enclaves on the Cape Flats, which, despite the (late) "rollout" of post-apartheid government housing remains as a highly visible reminder of the brutality of urban planning under apartheid. Earlier in 2015, the residents of Khayelitsha had protested the lack of waste and sewage disposal infrastructure, and, especially, the local (Democratic Alliance) government's stopgap measure of supplying the township with plastic portable toilets. Part of these so-called "poo protests" entailed launching excrement at tourists at the Cape Town International airport. Whatever one might think of the motivations behind this strategy, one has to grant that it was effective in getting both the media and the government's attention. Chumani Maxwele was a resident of Delft, a suburb adjoining Khayelitsha over the intersection of two major highways. For him the statue of Cecil John Rhodes, along with other tributes to colonial figures on campus, came to symbolize the "pain and hurt" black students were made to feel on a daily basis on a campus that through myriad ways, large and small, excluded and offended them.[17] Inspired by the Khayelitsha protests and fearing interference by the police or campus security, Maxwele decided to use a large annual arts festival called *Infecting the City* happening simultaneously at several spaces across Cape Town as occasion and cover for soiling the statue. While the idea to frame his action as "performance art" began as a pretense in order to avoid a vandalism charge, by the time the appointed day arrived, he took his artwork quite seriously:

> I would say that, as an artist, I did not need to be on the formal list of performing artists to produce art works that speak directly to the university's challenges of racism. With this sound justification, my fear evaporated. My placards were to read, "Exhibit White Arrogance @ UCT" and "Exhibit Black Assimilation @ UCT." I borrowed a drum from one of the very few black lecturers at UCT's music school. I had my pink makarapa (hard hat) and a whistle. I decided to perform topless in running tights and running shoes. This had to be a true performance.[18]

A *true* performance, perhaps, in the sense that it required the costume and props of a professional performance. But also in the sense of effective performativity, a performance that makes something happen, that institutes something in the world. This performance, however, was open-ended, not one for which the script was already written; no pre-existing convention dictated what it would achieve. There is a sense of surprise in Maxwele's account.[19] Even though Maxwele had planned his performance with the help of other students, this did not amount to a "movement" until the performance itself. It is only later that a terminology, "Black Pain," and a social media tag, #RhodesMustFall, would come into being.[20] The thinking, the initiatory gesture, was the performance itself, which was concrete and saturated with context, but also open to a movement, the form of which, to use a Derridean phrase, remained to come.

Maxwele's choice of target, which would attach a name to the movement, leading to sympathetic vibrations in Oriel College, Oxford, and at Harvard University, was to some extent contingent. It could just as easily have been the bust of the former Boer General and Prime Minister of South Africa, Jan Smuts. Or it could have been the steps or Hall named for Rhodes's crony, the Scots physician, politician, and colonial adventurer, Leander Starr Jameson. But the Rhodes statue was chosen for its central location and because students had already demanded that the statue be taken down the previous year. And Cecil John Rhodes does make for a fantastic emblem of colonialism. He was, at one point, the richest man in the world, an English robber baron, mining magnate, arch colonialist, who aligned his acquisition of vast personal wealth with what, to him and his contemporaries, no doubt seemed a nobler cause: the expansion and stabilization of the British Empire. His fervently espoused belief in colonialism, produced, among other odious quotations, this oft-cited, lapidary gem from a text Rhodes wrote in his 20s and shared with his friend and sometime-executor of his will, W.T. Stead: "I contend that we are the first race in the world, and that the more of the world we inhabit the better it is for the human race."[21]

Any number of statues, buildings, or artworks, not to mention policies or individuals, on the UCT campus are objectionable, or protestable, from the viewpoint of "Black Pain." The Cecil John Rhodes statue was chosen *as an example*, as illustrative of a greater principle: the university's ongoing colonial heritage. There is tension between, on the one hand, a Platonic tradition of exemplarity whereby example, or exemplar, is taken as a paragon, model, archetype, or a standard from which particulars are instantiated, and, on the other hand, an Aristotelian tradition whereby examples function in series, which, through a process of induction, allows for universals to be inferred. Alexander Gelley points out that the rhetoric of exemplarity frequently aims to alternate between these two philosophical traditions, "to mingle the singular with the normative, to mark an instance as fated."[22] Was #RhodesMustFall, as many of its detractors in the media claim it was, taking the Rhodes statue as the exemplar, the *nec plus ultra*, of the university and the country's colonial heritage, risking making a mountain of a molehill? Or was the movement, as it has regularly claimed, proposing the Rhodes statue simply as a particular, a part of the whole, a visible instance of the university's colonial legacy, which also, more urgently, but less iconically, entails a number of other facets which #RhodesMustFall have protested and advocated against? Whatever the intentions were, once the Rhodes statue was chosen, a name (or rather a hashtag) was assigned. There on March 9 under the aegis of *Infecting the City*, the die was cast: what may have been meant to be an exemplary instance, intended to lead from the particular to the general was nevertheless infected with singularity; Rhodes became an example, but also *the* example, of what the movement decreed "must fall."

One of the ironies of the debate about the statue that ensued is that those who argued the statue be retained, usually through some sort of compromise—the addition of a contextualizing plaque, its displacement to a less central location on campus, its removal to a museum, etc.—did so, by and large, as a caution against forgetting history,[23] and yet one of the consequences of #RhodesMustFall is that people, and especially journalists, are writing about Cecil John Rhodes more now than they have for decades. Given the frequency with which his name is evoked, Rhodes's life, his beliefs, the legacy he intended to leave, and the legacy he in fact did leave, should be under at least some critical scrutiny. Instead, the same potted biography is repeated in article after article.[24] For instance, while Rhodes's racism is undeniable, it is perhaps, from a twenty-first-century post-apartheid viewpoint, surprising in its character. In a newspaper interview, Chumani Maxwele argues for the appropriateness of his chosen target: "It is not just a statue, as many claim—Rhodes didn't want black people. Remember that, at some point, UCT also didn't want black people."[25] While Maxwele, a student of South African History and Politics, probably knows better, it is easy to take him to be implying that Rhodes didn't intend UCT to have black students. In fact, it was only in 1928 that UCT moved to its current site on the slopes of Table Mountain, which Rhodes never explicitly intended for a university, instead leaving his executors to determine its use on the condition that "any buildings which may be erected [on this property] shall be used exclusively for public purposes."[26] He does address education in his *Last Will and Testament*, extensively so in his stipulations for the Rhodes scholarships. But there he explicitly decrees: "No student shall be qualified or disqualified for election to a Scholarship on account of his race or religious opinions."[27] The archive of Rhodes's racism primarily come through two sources: 1) other people's records of his conversation, and 2) his actions. The latter, his racist actions, revealed largely, but not exclusively, in his colonial and mining concerns, speak louder than his racist words. But as Derrida reminds us in the context of apartheid, "there's no racism without a language. The point is not that acts of racial violence are only words but rather that they have to have a word."[28] What were the words and what was the language of Rhodes's racism?

While Rhodes has over the last year been regularly accused as a founder of apartheid *avant la lettre*, his racial vocabulary is distinct from that of the latter half of the twentieth century. Earlier I quoted a snippet reported by his friend W.T. Stead, which has been repeated in a slew of newspaper articles and on Rhodes's Wikipedia site, out of context, as the *quod erat demonstrandum* of his racism: "I contend that we are the first race in the world, and that the more of the world we inhabit the better it is for the human race."[29] One may be surprised to find that the "first race" in question, this exemplar of races in whose charge are the world's hopes for lasting peace and prosperity, is primarily defined by tongue rather than skin; it is the "English-speaking race," which, according to Rhodes's thinking, at least as reported by Stead, made a tragic misstep in allowing itself to become divided during the American war of Independence. In a fuzzy combination of misunderstood Darwinism, Biblical sentiment, an anti-Jingoistic Imperialism, and the militancy that derives from an Aristotelian ideal of Virtue, Rhodes set himself, and after his death the "secret society" he bequeathed, the task of re-uniting this English-speaking race for the grandiose purpose of world peace. Often decried or defended as (merely) a man of his times, Rhodes was rather a man living in the past, where those who spoke English could be thought of as a homogenous group. He did not consider the possibility of a monolingualism of the other,[30] which is to say a decoupling of, on the one hand, employing a language, knowing its codes and contexts, being capable of making utterances that are taken as meaningful, and, on the other hand, possessing a language or belonging to it. He did not, that is, understand the linguistic experience of the colonial subject (for example) or the *generic* tendency of language to defy and defer questions of origin. Rhodes's racism makes for a poor example. The words of Rhodes's racism are failed words, seeds that never found purchase; they are outdated, of course, in the sense that there is no obvious current group of racists espousing *these* ideas (which is not to say that there are no current racists who evoke his name), but they are also at once too nostalgic and too visionary to be said to belong to, or have been effective in, their own time. The same cannot be said about the medium of their expression, the language they aim to advance, which has, by all accounts, flourished. Could it be that, in the age of the "global Anglophone," Rhodes's simultaneously melancholy and proleptic linguistic racist project has finally been achieved, albeit in a manner he would find hard to recognize? And what would this mean for #RhodesMustFall, and especially for Fallism's *instantiations* outside of UCT?[31]

Setting Rhodes as the (bad) example means submitting to the logic of the example, one which, as Derrida argues in a piece on "The Law of Genre," is "a principle of contamination, a law of impurity, a parasitical economy," which is to say one whereby the singularity of the example always relies on but also threatens to overwhelm and infect the category it exemplifies.[32] It opens the question of the role of English, often taken as a language of national unity, as against Afrikaans, the infamous "language of the oppressor" in terms of the anti-apartheid struggle, and against other African languages. It suggests a return to colonialism as a category, which may be part of the driving force behind (re-) readings of Frantz Fanon, Ngũgĩ Wa Thiong'o, and Walter Mignolo with their very different senses of what de-colonization might entail. Doing so, it displaces the focus on "apartheid" and "post-apartheid," turning attention to persistent material inequalities, which both pre- and post-date apartheid, rather than the formal legal ones unique to it. It informs which parts of the world the movement might find resonance. In short, it participates in (is an example of) what Alexander Gelley calls the "scandal of example," whereby the reader or listener is forced to judge in the absence of a clear principle but on the basis of "the instance in its particularity" alone, therefore "continually and inescapably called upon to make judgments on insufficient grounds."[33]

The choice of setting and example clearly has a determining influence for a political project such as Fallism. In the age of the hashtag, this logic of political exemplarity has been generalized (if not quite universalized). The hashtag is derived from its use in social media where placing the noughts-and-crosses grid, usually called the "number" or "hash" sign, directly in front of a word or phrase (written without spaces or punctuation) makes that word or phrase searchable. This allows entries, or posts that contain this searchable "hashtag" (the phrase plus its hash sign), to be grouped together as part of a larger (open) textual unit. So a search for #RhodesMustFall on a social media platform will yield all the instances of people using that hashtag. In terms of sheer functionality, then, hashtags differ from both proper and common nouns, signifying neither a unique entity nor a class of entities. Hashtags have no unique, or even definite, referent (as would a proper noun); the referent of a hashtag is the history of its collective usage, which is always open to change. Rather than being *deduced* from a dictionary definition, and then applied to a phrase or word in its context (as one might do with a common noun), the meaning of a hashtag is *induced* from its many uses. They are for that reason not precisely declarative, stating, "This is" (RhodesMustFall, for example). They are instead cumulative, stating, "This *also* is" (RhodesMustFall, for example). Hashtags are by their nature too new to have fixed meanings; their malleability, reframe-ability, and reuse-ability is made operational through the hash before the phrase. Hashtags masquerade as examples, suggesting themselves as instances of a ruling principle. But there is no ruling principle, only the hashtag and its repetitions; we are always left to judge their meaning on insufficient grounds.

Interestingly, hashtags operate quite independently of the social media where they first became popular. The logic of the hashtag (if not its searchability) is transferable to a T-shirt, protest banner, or even into casual conversation without there ever having to be an actual (virtual) equivalent in cyberspace. I could, for example, punning on #PhilosophySoWhite, say to my family, "I was at the conference all day. #DerridaSoAfrican." And actually (virtually) existing hashtags do not need to tap into their searchability to function socially or semantically. I could post on Facebook: "Writing essay on 'Derrida as Figure in African Thought.' Conclusion: Derrida is not a figure in African thought and African thought does not figure in Derrida. #KiddingNotKidding." While #KiddingNotKidding is a perfectly useful hashtag expressing a complex juncture in our daily affective, epistemological, and cyber-political lives, its searchability is of small importance. This decoupling of the hashtag and social media (of the semantic functioning of the hashtag and its practical functionality as a searchable term online) is especially important in the South African context (for example), where a large number of people are aware of social media events without using social media themselves.[34] Newspapers, radio, television, word of mouth, graffiti, billboards, and even placards have an amplifying effect, extending the reach of the hashtag, and the exemplary logic of the hashtag, to people who rarely spend time on computers or smartphones. A giant billboard proclaiming "#ZumaMustFall" becomes legible as, "This is but one instance of a whole series of locutions declaring ZumaMustFall," even to people without any social media accounts.

In a South African idiom, the "must" of "MustFall," carries a valence that is somewhat different to its British or American counterparts. Possibly through linguistic interference from Afrikaans, the modal "must," while retaining its senses of obligation, necessity, and logical or deductive certainty, is above all used to express a strong recommendation bordering on a command. In South Africa, "must" is often heard in the second person. The uncanny thing about the hashtag wars over the past year is how effective they've been in making the thing that "must" happen actually happen. #RhodesMustFall almost immediately became a national talking point and soon we saw other things that must fall: #HeynekeMustFall (in reference to the former South African rugby coach), #DrinksCarriersMustFall (in reference to the dearth of black players in the South African national cricket team), #FeesMustFall (in reference to the national university fees protest of 2015 and 2016), and #ZumaMustFall (in reference to the president), for example. The Rhodes statue was taken down in a cathartic and carnivalesque scene on April 9, 2015. The Springbok coach resigned. The cricket team soon found two extremely promising young black players who immediately put in match-winning performances. The government acceded to not increasing university fees in 2016. And as for #ZumaMustFall, we'll have to wait and see. . . . But he *must*. Or at least he could. He could be recalled by the ANC; parliament could evoke section 102 of the Constitution and call for a motion of no confidence; the Constitutional Court could begin impeachment proceedings; or he could even, unlikely as it seems, resign of his own volition. In any of these cases we could in a fairly straightforward sense say, "Zuma has fallen." However, as Shakespeare and Derrida remind us, after the fall, the haunting begins; after demise or destruction, there is the question of how to inherit.[35]

An altogether stranger and perhaps more revealing instance of the recent "MustFall" hashtags is #MandelaMustFall. Not attached to one statue or object in particular, and never clear on what exactly Mandela's fall would look like after his death, this hashtag has been used for diverse purposes. On the one hand, the hashtag has been appropriated by relativist trolls proposing that statues commemorating Nelson Mandela in the United Kingdom should be subject to the same critique as are those commemorating Cecil Rhodes, on the grounds that they were both, in some sense, violent men. The more serious and compelling argument advanced under that hashtag is that Nelson Mandela's legacy is one of compromise, justice foregone, and betrayal in the name of reconciliation,[36] moreover that there is nothing sacrosanct in critiquing his presidency, which could do with some de-mythologizing.[37] The latter critique, which is by and large generational, and which has been advanced in the name of #RhodesMustFall and of the Economic Freedom Fighters (EFF), was perhaps foreshadowed by Chumani Maxwele in his initial comments on his performance. The South-African online newspaper, *The Journalist*,[38] reports Maxwele saying, "We acknowledge our parents' achievements fighting against apartheid but we are saying now it is about time for us to reflect on our pain, our suffering collectively."[39] In this spirit, to say #MandelaMustFall is to say the urgency of inequality, of injustice, and of the black subject's pain requires us to look past or be willing to critique the ideals of non-racialism (a liberal tool for keeping the status quo intact) and reconciliation (which has only ever protected and enabled white privilege) that Mandela has come to stand for, to be *exemplary* of. Mandela: a leader who has left his people materially worse off in the name of liberal principle. This characterization of Mandela still has quite some way to go before matching the sheer villainy of Rhodes in his most recent potted mini-biographies (meant, of course, to counterbalance the imperial heroism of his statuary representations);[40] even given his failings, it seems bizarre that Mandela and Rhodes should be subjected to the same censure, condemned to the same "fall." And yet Fallists are not the first to decide to group these two men together: *The Mandela Rhodes Foundation* has been offering scholarships since 2005 for "candidates who identify with the values set out by Mr. Mandela and Mr. Rhodes."[41] Mandela and Rhodes would seem to have mutual admirers as well as mutual detractors.

Those of us who wish to keep the legacies of Rhodes and Mandela firmly distinct, however, could do worse than turn to Jacques Derrida's "Admiration of Nelson Mandela, Or, the Laws of Reflection." Derrida's text focuses on Mandela's testimony at his 1962 and 1964 trials, speeches that come to Derrida in written form, as texts or testaments which he inherits and from which he asks others to inherit. There is a long gap between Mandela's 1962 and 1964 speeches, Derrida's 1986 text, and the #MandelaMustFall hashtag, but read together now they seem especially responsive to each other, even against the flow of time, each posing the question of legacy and inheritance: colonial inheritance and Mandela's own legacy. For Derrida,

> There are at least two ways of receiving a testament [. . .] One can inflect it toward what *bears witness* only to a past and knows itself condemned to reflecting that which will not return: a kind of West in general, the end of a race that is also the trajectory from a luminous source, the close of an epoch, for example that of the Christian West (Mandela speaks its language, he is also an English Christian). But, another inflection, if the testament is always made in front of witnesses, a witness in front of witnesses, it is also so as to open and to enjoin, it is to confide in others the responsibility of a future.[42]

So, for Derrida, when Mandela becomes a lawyer and inherits the law,[43] it remains a question whether the law is "essentially a thing of the West" or whether "its formal universality retains some irreducible link with European or even Anglo-American history."[44] According to Derrida, Mandela *admires* this law, both valuing it and casting a reflective gaze on it, but without accepting it as entirely foreign or entirely ideal.

> What [Mandela's] fascination seems to bring into view here, what mobilizes and immobilizes Mandela's attention, is not only parliamentary democracy, whose principle presents itself *for example but not exemplarily* in the West. It is the already virtually accomplished passage, if one can say this, from parliamentary democracy to revolutionary democracy: a society without class and without private property. We have just encountered, then, a supplementary paradox: the *effective* accomplishment, the fulfillment of the democratic form, the *real* determination of the formality, will only have taken place in the past of this non-Western society [. . .].[45]

It is this manner of reflection, in the future perfect, strikingly lacking in the Fallist perspective, that we can learn to inherit from Derrida and Mandela. Like the so-called "West," Derrida's South Africa also "presents itself *for example but not exemplarily;*" it is both "the most singular" place and just one part metonymically standing for, and *"deciding,"* the whole. This form of reflection, which is also a form of admiration, avoids the peril of narcissism that haunts every inward looking act. While some readers of Derrida would agree with Tom Cohen that Derrida's later texts reveal a "closet affirmation of Eurocentrism,"[46] and that future scholars looking back will be "pissed, and probably dismissive about the moaning about legacies, mourning, ghosts, and so on,"[47] an attentive reading of "Admiration of Nelson Mandela" would suggest otherwise. The response that Derrida finds to Eurocentrism, to European law (or rather, in this case of that hyphenation Rhodes would universalize, to "Anglo-American" law) in Mandela's admiration is one that manages to inherit and critique at the same time. It is an approach to de-colonization that disaggregates brute interest and repression from a humanist legacy that was never exclusively proper to Europe, or Anglo-America, in the first place, and whereby "places," like "South Africa" (for example), stand in metonymic relation to a yet-to-be-determined, larger, global whole.[48]

#RhodesMustFall has militated against current and ongoing colonial structures, bound together by the experience of "black pain" and the group-affirming rhetoric of taking offense, politically mobilized as a collective body in the physical destruction of symbolic vestiges of an older colonialism found in the form of statues and artworks. All of this requires emphasis on a group identity derived from embodied experience of a singular history and a singular place. But as a hashtag, and as a now-international movement whose strategies and discourse exist in relation to a network of other international hashtag movements, such as #BlackLivesMatter (for example), #RhodesMustFall already has to think of itself as also existing in a context other than the one suggested by the narcissistic closure of singularity, inaccessibility, and untranslatability, that is, as one example among others and as being in relation to the world, including the Western world. Nelson Mandela's admiration, in Derrida's reading, gives the possibility of seeing the seeds of a South-African philosophy in European/Anglo-American law and of seeing the flourishing of those seeds as taking place in the future, on African soil (for example), cultivated by future generations. As a response to the world to which #RhodesMustFall is also a response, it is exemplary.

NOTES

1. Nicholas Royle, *Jacques Derrida* (Cambridge: Polity, 2003).
2. Simon Glendinning, *Derrida: A Very Short Introduction* (Oxford: OUP, 2011).
3. Ibid., 1.
4. Benoît Peeters, *Derrida: A Biography*, trans. Andrew Brown (Cambridge: Polity, 2013), 2.
5. Jacques Derrida, "Racism's Last Word," trans. Peggy Kamuf, *Critical Inquiry* 12 (1985): 290-299.
6. Jacques Derrida, *Specters of Marx: The State of Debts, The Work of Mourning and the New International*, trans. Peggy Kamuf (New York: Routledge, 1994).
7. Jacques Derrida, "On Forgiveness," in *On Cosmopolitanism and Forgiveness*, trans. Michael Hughes (New York: Routledge, 2001), 27-60.
8. Carl Schmitt, *Political Theology: Four Chapters on the Concept of Sovereignty*, trans. George Schwab (Chicago: University of Chicago Press, 2005): 5.

9. *Derrida*, directed by Kirby Dick and Amy Ziering Kofman (New York: Zeitgeist Films, 2002), DVD.
10. Ibid.
11. Ibid.
12. Kirby Dick and Amy Ziering Kofman, "DERRIDA–Screenplay" in *Derrida: Screenplay and Essays on the Film*, ed. Kirby Dick and Amy Ziering Kofman (New York: Routledge, 2005): 91.
13. Rob Nixon and Anne McClintock's "No Names Apart" (1986), a polemic, written when its South-African authors were still graduate students at Columbia University, against Derrida's "quarantine" of the term apartheid "from historical process" in "Racism's Last Word," seems to have been motivated by a similar defensive ire at the foreigner daring to cast his regard on South African matters without being able to account for all its local complexity or nuance. Anne McClintock and Rob Nixon, "No Names Apart: The Separation of Word and History in Derrida's '*Le Dernier mot du racisme*'," *Critical Inquiry* 13, no. 1 (1986): 141.
14. Disputed, for example, by Achille Mbembe who attempts a high wire act in reinterpreting Fanon for members of the movement in public lectures and conversations with student activists on the UCT campus, the University of the Witwatersrand campus, as well as at Stellenbosch University, producing a reading that is meant to *educate* student activists, providing correctives to their casual versions of Fanon's thought without simply resting on the authority of the teacher, attempting "an entirely different form of address—one that could speak both to reason and to affect." See Achille Mbembe, *Decolonizing Knowledge and the Question of the Archive* (Africa is a Country, 2016), eBook, https://africaisacountry.atavist.com/decolonizing-knowledge-and-the-question-of-the-archive
15. See, for instance, the essays gathered as responses to Derrida's *Specters of Marx* in *Ghostly Demarcations* (New York: Verso, 2008).
16. E.C. Eze and Bruce Janz, "Jacques Derrida, 1930-2004," *Philosophia Africana* 8, no. 1 (2005): 81.
17. "Newsmaker–Chumani Maxwele: No regrets for throwing faeces at Rhodes statue" in *City Press 2015-03-29*.
18. Chumani Maxwele, "Black Pain Led Me to Throw Rhodes Poo," *Business Day*, March 16, 2016.
19. "*Suddenly*, the Cape Times and e.tv were there, and people started gathering around, asking questions about the political art." Ibid., my emphasis.
20. "It was a performance that was to last the whole day. By midday, other black students had joined me and there, on that day, March 9, 2015, the #RhodesMustFall student movement was born out of pain and frustration—what we later called Black Pain." Ibid.
21. Cecil John Rhodes, *The Last Will and Testament of Cecil John Rhodes with Elucidatory Notes to which Are Added Some Political and Religious Ideas of the Testator*, ed. W. T. Stead (London: William Clowes and Sons, 1902), 58-59.
22. Alexander Gelley, *Unruly Examples: On the Rhetoric of Exemplarity* (Stanford: Stanford University Press, 1995), 2.
23. After Maxwele's protest and before the removal of the Rhodes statue, the former anti-apartheid activist and South African constitutional court judge, Albie Sachs, for instance, suggested: "Instead of extinguishing Rhodes, we should keep him alive on the campus and force him, even if posthumously, to witness surroundings that tell him and the world that he is now living in a constitutional democracy. . . . Instead of trying to obliterate our history, we need to honour those who had struggled for justice, and transform the area by setting University Press a dialogue between the past and present." Albie Sachs, "The Rhodes Debate: How We Can Have the Last Laugh," *University of Cape Town News*, March 30, 2015, https://www.uct.ac.za/dailynews/?id=9064.
24. To give a negative example—an example of a bad trend—always seems unfair, like an act of scapegoating. What follows is Mark Gevisser's entirely typical descrip-

tion of Rhodes. Gevisser is no better or worse than most commentator's in this respect. I choose him as an example on the same principle as the implicit rule of satirical commentary: always punch up. Gevisser's well-earned reputation can take the punch. "The British-born Rhodes, who died in 1902, is the father of the modern South African state and its most identifiable symbol of colonial depredation. As an industrialist, he pioneered the diamond and gold industry; as a politician, he codified the system of racial domination that would become known as apartheid. This was the man who said of the British that 'we are the first race in the world' and who wrote that if there were a God, 'he would like me ... to paint as much of the map of Africa British Red as possible.'" Mark Gevisser, "South African Students Must Take Movement to Society for Real Progress," *Los Angeles Times*, April 18, 2015, http://www.latimes.com/opinion/op-ed/la-oe-0419-gevisser-rhodes-20150419-story.html.

25. "Newsmaker–Chumani Maxwele: No regrets for throwing faeces at Rhodes statue," *City Press*, March 29, 2015, *http://www.news24.com/Archives/City-Press/Newsmaker-Chumani-Maxwele-No-regrets-for-throwing-faeces-at-Rhodes-statue-20150429*.

26. Rhodes, *Last Will and Testament*, 13.

27. Ibid., 39.

28. Jacques Derrida, "Racism's Last Word," trans. Peggy Kamuf, *Critical Inquiry* 12, no. 1 (1985): 292.

29. Rhodes, *Final Will and Testament*, 58-59.

30. See Jacques Derrida, *Monolingualism of the Other, Or, The Prosthesis of Origin*, trans. Patrick Mensah (Stanford, CA: Stanford University Press, 1998).

31. Take, for example, #OpenStellenbosch, a movement at Stellenbosch University, an institution which has, until very recently, been taken to *exemplify* higher education in Afrikaans. #OpenStellenbosch was directly inspired by #RhodesMustFall and, in fact, initially bore the rather awkward name, #MatiesMustFall. At its inaugural meeting, at the urging of a Senior Lecturer in the *English* department of a traditionally Afrikaans university, an Afrikaans-speaking Shakespeare expert, it was determined that for the movement it would be the Afrikaans language that would act as "our Rhodes statue."

32. Jacques Derrida, "The Law of Genre," trans. Avital Ronell, *Critical Inquiry* 7, no.1 (1980): 59.

33. Gelley, 14.

34. Ian Glenn warns that when scholars and critics discuss #RhodesMustFall, "an over-emphasis on social media neglects the crucial roles played by broadcast media, print journalism and closed social media communications such as WhatsApp." He is no doubt right. I would add that (in addition to supplementing our analyses with considerations of media platforms beyond Twitter) we also need to consider the form and rhetorical effect of the hashtag when decoupled from its native platform: the way that the hashtag functions when employed outside of social media. Ian Glenn, "Rhodes Must Fall (#RMF) and Fees Must Fall (#FMF)," *Bulletin of the National Library of South Africa* 70, no. 1 (2016): 83.

35. Derrida, *Specters of Marx*, 8.

36. Ian Glenn notes that among "young educated urban African people"—i.e., the primary constituency of #RhodesMustFall and #FeesMustFall—a "common motif is a suspicion of the Constitution ('an instrument of repression') and of Mandela's compromise and Mandela as compromiser." Glenn, "Rhodes Must Fall," 89. Mark Gevisser, writing after Maxwele's protest performance but before the statue's removal, attributes the #RhodesMustFall movement even more directly to Mandela: "South Africa's negotiated settlement between blacks and whites, led by Nelson Mandela, meant that Rhodes and many other colonial- and apartheid-era figures could remain on their plinths. Twenty years later, it is indeed time for this society to reconsider their presence on the South African landscape." Gevisser, "South African Students Must Take Movement to Society for Real Progress." From this perspective, the attack on the Rhodes statue was always already an attack on Mandela (whose own statues, all over South Africa, now dominate communal and commercial spaces alike).

37. Already in 2004, Grant Farred and Rita Barnard guest editing a special edition of the *South Atlantic Quarterly* dealing with (as the subtitle indicates) "A Decade of Post-Apartheid South Africa" opted for the telling title, "After the Thrill Is Gone." Farred in his contribution to that volume notes that this title is meant to take "the narrative of 'progress' from a racist past to a nonracial present (and future)," which had been "a critical modality [with] significant purchase in the post-1994 society," and displace that narrative with "a ruptured, critical, discontented relationship to the present." Grant Farred, "The Not Yet Counterpartisan: A New Politics of Oppositionality," *South Atlantic Quarterly* 103, no. 4 (2004): 592-93. More than a decade later, the South-African present remains "post-apartheid" (though "de-colonial" has become an important alternative formulation), and the narrative of progress, tied to the figure of Nelson Mandela and his "Madiba magic," has become even less credible.

38. The newspaper's slogan is perhaps worth mentioning here: "Context Matters."

39. See: http://www.thejournalist.org.za/spotlight/we-love-uct-says-student-who-covered-rhodes-in-shit

40. This one, for example, distorting and defamiliarizing Rhodes's own racial discourse: "Cecil Rhodes belonged to *the race of men* who were convinced that to be black is a liability. During his time and life in Southern Africa, he used his considerable power–political and financial–to make black people all over Southern Africa pay a bloody price for his beliefs." Mbembe, *Decolonizing Knowledge and the Question of the Archive*, my emphasis.

41. "Guiding Principles," *The Mandela Rhodes Foundation*, Accessed May 18, 2017, http://mandelarhodes.org/the-scholarship/guiding-principles/

42. Jacques Derrida, "Admiration of Nelson Mandela, or The Laws of Reflection," trans. Charles Gelman, *Law & Literature* 26, no. 1 (2014): 82.

43. In South Africa there is a distinction between two kinds of lawyer: advocates and attorneys. While Mandela passed the admission exam to practice as an attorney in 1952, he did not in fact obtain his LLB degree (which qualified him to act as an advocate) until almost forty years later. In his excellent piece about Mandela's long legal education, Adam Sitze writes, "Between 1939, when Mandela began studying administrative law at the University of Fort Hare, and 1989, when Mandela finally received his LLB degree through correspondence from the University of South Africa (UNISA), Mandela would enroll in no fewer than fifty courses in law at four different universities. For fully half a century, Nelson Mandela was, in a sense we yet have fully to comprehend, a student of law." Adam Sitze, "Mandela and the Law," in *The Cambridge Companion to Nelson Mandela*, ed. Rita Barnard (Cambridge: Cambridge University Press, 2016), 134. There is an important sense, then, in which Mandela was not only, as Derrida would have it, a *"man of law"* both *"by vocation"* and *"by profession."* Derrida, "Admiration of Nelson Mandela," 18. Mandela was also, for half a century, a *student of law*, a student in university systems far more colonial and unjust than those currently under protest.

44. Ibid., 65.

45. Ibid., 72.

46. Tom Cohen, "Reading: Derrida and the Non-Future," in *Jacques Derrida: Key Concepts*, ed. Claire Colebrook (London: Routledge, 2014), 154.

47. Ibid., p155

48. "Some would be tempted to see in Mandela a witness or a martyr to the past [...]But the contrary can be said: his reflection allows us to glimpse—in the most singular geopolitical conjuncture, in that extreme concentration of the whole history of humanity which today are places or stakes named, for example, 'South Africa' or 'Israel'—the promise of what still has never been seen, nor heard, in a law that has presented itself in the West, at the limit of the West, only to slip away from it just as soon. That which will be decided in these 'places' so named,—which are also formidable metonyms—would decide all, if there were still that—some all." Derrida, "Admiration of Nelson Mandela," 27.

WORKS CITED

Cohen, Tom. "Reading: Derrida and the Non-Future." *Jacques Derrida: Key Concepts.* Edited by Claire Colebrook, 154-165. London: Routledge, 2014.
Derrida, Jacques. "The Law of Genre." Translated Avital Ronell. *Critical Inquiry* 7, no.1 (1980): 55-81.
———. "Racism's Last Word." Translated by Peggy Kamuf. *Critical Inquiry* 12 (1985): 290-299.
———. *Specters of Marx: The State of Debts, the Work of Mourning and the New International.* Translated by Peggy Kamuf. New York: Routledge, 1994.
———. *Monolingualism of the Other, Or, The Prosthesis of Origin.* Translated by Patrick Mensah. Stanford, CA: Stanford University Press, 1998.
———. *On Cosmopolitanism and Forgiveness.* Translated by Michael Hughes. New York: Routledge, 2001.
———. "Admiration of Nelson Mandela, or The Laws of Reflection." Translated by Charles Gelman. *Law & Literature* 26, no. 1 (2014): 9-30.
Dick, Kirby and Amy Ziering Kofman. *Derrida: Screenplay and Essays on the Film.* Edited by Kirby Dick and Amy Ziering Kofman. New York: Routledge, 2005.
Farred, Grant. "The Not Yet Counterpartisan: A New Politics of Oppositionality." *South Atlantic Quarterly* 103, no. 4 (2004): 589-605.
Gelley, Alexander. *Unruly Examples: On the Rhetoric of Exemplarity.* Stanford: Stanford University Press, 1995.
Glendinning, Simon. *Derrida: A Very Short Introduction.* Oxford: OUP, 2011.
Glenn, Ian. "Rhodes Must Fall (#RMF) and Fees Must Fall (#FMF)." *Bulletin of the National Library of South Africa* 70, no. 1 (2016): 83-97.
McClintock, Anne and Rob Nixon. "No Names Apart: The Separation of Word and History in Derrida's '*Le Dernier mot du racisme*'." *Critical Inquiry* 13, no. 1 (1986): 140-54.
Peeters, Benoît. *Derrida: A Biography.* Translated by Andrew Brown. Cambridge: Polity, 2013.
Rhodes, Cecil John. *The Last Will and Testament of Cecil John Rhodes with Elucidatory Notes to which Are Added Some Political and Religious Ideas of the Testator.* Edited by W. T. Stead. London: William Clowes and Sons, 1902.
Royle, Nicholas. *Jacques Derrida.* Cambridge: Polity, 2003.
Schmitt, Carl. *Political Theology: Four Chapters on the Concept of Sovereignty.* Translated by George Schwab. Chicago: University of Chicago Press, 2005.
Sitze, Adam. "Mandela and the Law." *The Cambridge Companion to Nelson Mandela.* Edited by Rita Barnard, 134-61. Cambridge: Cambridge University Press, 2016.

FIVE

Jacques Derrida as an African Philosopher

Some Considerations from Francophone African Philosophy

Kasereka Kavwahirehi

We can approach the theme of "Derrida as an African philosopher" from various angles. I have chosen to approach it by way of a small detour that can shed light on certain aspects, which while not directly related, are no less significant. In fact, I will try to approach this issue by inscribing it within the history of Francophone African philosophy and by stressing the meaning of the adjective "African" which not only refers to a question of identity (who is or who can be called *African* philosopher?) but also to the place from which someone thinks or the question of philosophy is raised. Hence two possible questions: what does it mean to be an *African* philosopher? and what does it mean to practice philosophy *from* or *in a place* called "Africa?".[1]

Of the two questions, the last is certainly the most challenging as it suggests that some connections exist between philosophy and territory, or, rather, between philosophy and geography.[2] This assertion can be challenged especially if one considers that philosophy is concerned with abstraction and universals. But asserting that there is some connection between philosophy and territory as Deleuze and Guattari do in *What is Philosophy?*[3] or between philosophy and place, precisely the place where "the question of the right to philosophy takes place,"[4] does not mean to dilute "philosophy's traditional (although never completely fulfilled) striving universals."[5] It is a way to remind that "thinking is neither a line drawn between subject and object nor a revolving of one around the other. Rather, thinking takes place in the relationship of territory and the earth."[6] Deleuze goes farther by saying that geography is not only internal to philosophy, to the point that it overlaps to form a lexical compound that can be dubbed "geophilosophy," it opens a horizontal, or more precisely, a diagonal plane that dissects the vertical, more canonical one formed by historical sequence. Needless to say, as Roberto Esposito notes,

> Deleuze's reference to earth does not allude to the fixity of a picture frozen in time, or to the inevitability of ethnic or even anthropological roots. On the contrary, it implies a complex dialectic in which the territory is only one pole, opposed by a corresponding, simultaneous movement of deterritorialization: an outwardly-turning movement that breaks up territorial boundaries.[7]

In other words, placing philosophy in a geography is a way of paying attention to the conditions of possibility of the question of philosophy, or "the question of the right to philosophy," a question which, due to their cultural, political and intellectual history, is crucial for postcolonial Africans. As Janz precisely puts it in *Philosophy in an African Place*:

> (. . .) The fact is, no philosophy is from nowhere. Philosophy always comes from a place, and that place is never completely covered by abstraction. It is never irrelevant, even if it has been ignored. Not that there is some necessary causal connection or geographical determinism, as if by figuring out the place from which philosophy comes, we can encapsulate it, know it, and need to attend to its actual content. Place is a far more complex notion than what can be contained in geography. Philosophy is not reducible to place, there is no genetic fallacy or geographical determinism here. Philosophy remains a reflection on its place, geographically, culturally, disciplinarily, and intellectually.[8]

Janz actually goes farther, stating rightly "African philosophy is a particularly good context in which to take this task . . . since (whether its practitioners put it in explicit terms or not) it is consumed with its place in the world of philosophy in general, its place in relation to its cultural origins and present milieu, its place in formation of the identification of its practitioners."[9] Thus the signification of my title: by "Derrida as African Philosophy" I want to explore how the French philosopher, born in Algeria, can be located in Francophone African philosophy, that is, the philosophical tradition developed from Africa. I will do this by examining how African philosophy/philosopher tried to define it/himself and illustrated what is to do philosophy in African place or what kind of questions are raised from this place

WHO CAN BE CONSIDERED AS AN *AFRICAN* PHILOSOPHER?

To answer this question, the classical text by Paulin Hountondji, provides a useful point of entry. In fact, in *African Philosophy Myth and Reality*, Hountondji defines African philosophy as "a set of texts, specifically the set of texts written by Africans and described as philosophical by their authors themselves."[10]

If one considers this definition, which was but a starting point for Hountondji, there are two things worth highlighting. The existence of African philosophy today is no longer an issue. Many texts of a higher philosophical quality as well as African scholarly journals dedicated to philosophy exist. However, what seems problematic and will thus be the focus of my reflection, is what Hountondji means by "African" or "an *African* philosopher." Who is African and what does it mean to be an African philosopher today? To answer this question, the chapter which Hountondji devotes to Antoine Guillaume Amo, an "African" whose education and philosophical career all took place in eighteenth-century Germany, seems critique. What interests me specifically is the way Hountondji chose to justify the qualification of Antoine Guillaume Amo as "an African philosopher."

> Axim is an old African town situated on the "Gulf of Guinea," in present-day south-west Ghana, not far from the Ivorian frontier. It was there, in the first years of the eighteenth century, that the black philosopher was born who signed himself in Latin Amo-Guinea-Afer or Amo Guiena-Africanus (Amo the Guinean), as though he was afraid that his long European adventure might make him or his circle forget his African origins and ties.
>
> Amo's philosophical career took place principally in Germany, where he received a training that he in turn was destined to dispense as a teacher in the Universities of Halle, Wittenberg and Jena between the years 1730 and 1740, before returning to his home country where he died.[11]

In this description, one can note the emphasis placed on geographic location on the one hand, and on the other, on "African ties." According to Hountondji, these ties manifest themselves, amongst other ways, through Amo's signature (*Amo Guinea-Africanus*) and, above all, the fact that he chose to return to Ghana, which he had left very young, to end his days. Thus, even if his academic and philosophical career unfolded primarily in Germany and even if the issues he dealt with were those in vogue in his German environment, which means that they did not support any claim of specificity tied to his African origin, Antoine Guillaume Amo "was and remained, in origin and in personal destiny," an African philosopher.[12] It is interesting to point out that in *Lies that Bind. Rethinking Identity*, Kwame Anthony Appiah adds another argument. He suggests that "when Johann Gottfried Krauss, the Rector of Wittenberg, complimented Dr. Amo on his successful defense of his dissertation, he began by talking about his African background, mentioning some of the most famous African writers from Antiquity, including the Roman playwright Terence—who, like Amo, had given himself the last name Afer—and Tertullian and St. Augustine, along with other Fathers of the Church born in North Africa. He mentioned the Moors who conquered Spain from Africa."[13] As Appiah makes it clear, among the thinkers mentioned by Kraus, none "would have had dark skin or tightly curled black hair like Amo's."[14] Then, one could hardly believe that Kraus and his contemporaries were interested in a question about Africans but about black people or Negroes. And to solve this question, the right way would be to link Amo to the philosophical tradition of Timbuktu,[15] that even Hountondji ignored.

However, while recognizing him as an African philosopher and finding in him a model for Africans who should also "freely seize the whole existing philosophical and scientific heritage, assimilating and mastering it in order to be able to transcend it"[16], Hountondji expresses disappointment on one point: the exclusive insertion of Amo's work in a non-African theoretical or intellectual tradition.

> Amo the African wrote in Latin for a European public, could be read and possibly appreciated, discussed, criticized only by that European public. He forged his own problematic from themes and concepts integral to the history of European philosophy and contributed by his work to enrichment of that history at a time when there was no comparable theoretical tradition in his own country.[17]

While acknowledging that Amo could do little else, being the victim of historical circumstance, Hountondji writes:

> Our disappointment concerns not the content of Amo's work but its social insertion. What we regret about the work of this *African* philosopher (for African he was and remained, in origin and in personal destiny, he who voluntarily returned to his people after his long European adventure and ended his days among them), is that it belongs entirely to a non-African theoretical *tradition.*[18]

In other words, for Hountondji, if African origin and ties to the African continent or to the fate of the continent and its people are enough for a philosopher to be classified as African, he nevertheless implies that the African philosopher should not get caught in the trap of extraversion, that is to say he should not just take part, as an individual, in the major scientific debates of the industrialized world. His duty is to participate in the progressive creation in African countries of structures for dialogue and debate indispensable to the existence of science and African scientific or theoretical tradition. It is precisely on this point that Hountondji's position can lead us to ask a number of questions.

Of course, readers of Houtondji are familiar with the place that criticism of extraversion of African discourse occupies in his work. Readers also understand that the insistence upon Guillaume Amo's origin and ties to Africa on the one hand and regret over the exclusive insertion of Amo's work in a non-African theoretical tradition on the other hand, echoes the distinction that Marxists made between "speech from within" and "speech from without."[19] In Houtondji's case, 'speech from within' is discourse that is not only socially and theoretically inserted in Africa, but is also produced by those of African origin. But what Hountondji seems to have forgotten or minimized is that, as V.Y. Mudimbe points out, many foreign scholars such as the Belgian missionary Placid Tempels and Dominique Nothomb, who took part in the transformation of discourse paradigms on Africa and in Africa, actually were or are African at heart and often by choice. It is therefore problematic to exclude contributions made to African philosophy by anyone of foreign origin.

The problem becomes apparent when we consider the history of ideas in Africa since *Bantu Philosophy* by the Belgian missionary Placid Tempels, to authors of African origin such as Bimwenyi Kweshi as well as Alexis Kagame, John Mbiti and Vincent Mulago. Indeed, as Mudimbe highlights: "When one considers that Kagame is Tempels's disciple and that Mbiti and Bimwenyi represent a dialectical effort of going beyond Tempels' discourse, the distinction becomes wholly questionable."[20] The paradox is that by writing a book intended first for missionaries, Placid Tempels initiated African debates on the existence of an African philosophy, creating a split between those for and against his book. The evolution of African philosophy as we know it is incomprehensible without *Bantu Philosophy*. It seems difficult to say that the central book in the development of African philosophy does not belong to this field of study for the simple reason that its author is of Belgian origin. If colonial history is not a sheer parenthesis in African histories, rather a part of African histories—Africans cannot understand themselves and their social and intellectual environment without referring to it[21]—it would be nonsense to not consider *Bantu Philosophy* as a part of philosophical African tradition in the making.

V.Y. MUDIMBE AND "J.-P. SARTRE AS AN AFRICAN PHILOSOPHER"

Considering this limit of Hountondji's perspective, Mudimbe's provocative metaphor of "J. P. Sartre as an African Philosopher" or, more so, as "Negro Philosopher" opens new horizons that can be explored. First, Mudimbe's bold move is of great significance because it leads us to rethink and call into question what has separated us during the last three centuries, namely the classification of races, the division of humanity into camps based on skin color or autochthony,[22] and to imagine a great brotherhood beyond the classificatory modes of thought inherited from the Enlightenment.[23] But this act also underscores, on the one hand, Sartre's role in propagating Negritude and, on the other hand, the fact that he was the first to identify methods for interpreting the metaphors of black poets, to name the rules for the modulation of action, to finally establish a formulation of the claims of the French scholars with black skin and to propose a universal strategy. "It is Sartre who in 1948," writes Mudimbe, "with his essay, *Black Orpheus*, an introduction to Senghor's *Anthology of New Negro and Malagasy Poetry*, transformed Negritude into a major political event and a philosophical criticism of colonialism."[24]

But Mudimbe does not carry out a simple apologia for Sartre's intellectual generosity nor does he underestimate the political value of his act. He remains fully aware of the ambiguity that accompanied the act of raising the French existentialist to the rank of philosopher of the Negritude movement. On the one hand, Sartre's intervention guaranteed the philosophical legitimacy of Negritude discourse, but on the other hand, it marked, by its ambiguity, the precise limits of the emergence and launching of the Negro cry. On the one hand, "Sartre presents means for a struggle against the dominant ideology and affirms the right of African to fashion a new mode of thought, of speech, and life, and he sets up paradigms that would allow the colonized black to assume control of a self."[25] But, on the other hand, he shows how Negritude is dialectically made to destroy itself: "it is an antithetical moment that only another bedazzlement (*éblouissement*) can follow." Mudimbe continues: "But the antithesis is also remarkably Sartre's text: his *Black Orpheus* displaces the aims of the rebellion of young French scholars with black skin."[26] In this regard, it is worth noting Frantz Fanon's irritation after reading *Black Orpheus*, even if, some years later, he had to recognize the validity of the Sartrean dialectical principle by stating in *The Wretched of the Earth* that there will be no black culture—the black problem being a political problem.

Despite the ambiguity of Sartre's intervention, it seems impossible to deny that *Black Orpheus* was "a major ideological moment, perhaps one of the most important" whose impact went beyond the black world. Sartre, an anti-colonial philosopher, broadened the horizon of the emancipation struggles of the colonized. Indeed, Mudimbe writes:

> (*Black Orpheus*) displays both the potentialities of Marxist revolution and the negation of colonialism and racism . . . What Sartre did was to impose philosophically the political dimension of negativity in the colonial history. This was a compelling task for Africans. By emphasizing the relativity and the sins of Western expansionism, he gave meaning and credibility to all signs of opposition to colonialism and called for a new understanding of significance of violence in the colonies. Thus, Pan-African Conference, Gandhi's noncooperation movement, and the

Neo-Dastur party emerging in Tunisia would appear to have a dialectical and positive portent for the future: they could influence the lives of the colonized and, also fundamentally, provide the possibility of new societies.[27]

Important from an ideological perspective, Sartre's short treatise also carries crucial epistemological significance. Indeed, by rejecting both "the colonial rationale and the set of culturally eternal values as bases for society, *Black Orpheus* philosophically posited a relativist perspective for African social studies." While we cannot say with certainty that Sartre necessarily influenced Georges Balandier, whose works *Sociologie des Brazzavilles noirs*[28] and *Sociologie actuelle de l'Afrique noire* mark a shift in ways of discussing the African experience; even if he did not serve as a guide to all African thinkers, it remains true that

> (H)is insights illuminated the trends and preoccupations of African scholarship. His path to liberation meant of a new epistemological configuration under the sovereignty of dialectical reason . . . It is from his interpretation, rather than from communism, that the two characteristics of present-day African studies presented by Copans make sense: on the one hand, a radical criticism of imperialism and, on the other, a "Marxist revival" which, in effect, has taken hold of the whole theoretical domain of African studies.[29]

As we can see, with his metaphor Mudimbe aptly describes the reality that overemphasis on African origin of a thinker could conceal. Given the context of its emergence, we cannot define African philosophy solely by geographical origins of authors without somewhat obscuring the history of its development. It seems that more than geographic location, the place from which we speak, the place from which the question of philosophy or, rather, the place in which or from which the question of the right to philosophy takes place, could perhaps be a better criterion for defining African philosophy/philosopher. But it is important to remind us here that what we mean by place, with its geographic, cultural, disciplinary, and intellectual complexity, is neither a physical location to which philosophy could be reduced, nor "so much a specific geographical area encompassed within stable boundaries, as a set of environmental, linguistic, 'tonal' characteristics connoting a specific mode that is unmistakable when compared to other styles of thought."[30]

Needless to say, by taking this position, I expose myself to criticism from champions of that which is "authentically African." I am referring here to the sort of criticism that the French literary critic Michel Hauser expresses toward Negritude.[31] After having brought to light numerous Western influences on Negritude (The Bible, anthropological texts, Baudelaire, Lautréamont, Rimbaud, Mallarmé, Valéry, Claudel, etc.), Hauser not only casts doubt upon its authenticity but rejects the movement's revolutionary character. Thus, following Michel Hausser, one could also say that because of Sartre's influence, and why not mention the influences of Marx, Paul Ricoeur, Michel Foucault, Althusser, on Hountondji, Mudimbe, etc., African philosophy is not authentically African. This seems somewhat excessive and regressive. It is more appropriate to concentrate on the fact that, despite the ambiguity of his intervention in the fate of Negritude, "Sartre as an African philosopher" or as "Negro philosopher," reveals the dialogic, intercultural and open nature of the field of African philosophy. African philosophy does not arise, in a deterministic fashion, geographic origin or something timeless and elusive that would define what is authentically African. If we decide to take the African origin of an idea or a movement seriously as a discriminating factor, we should not forget that Africa is, as Mudimbe states in *Tales of Faith. Religion as Political Performance,* an *"espace métissé,"* and the debate on African philosophy is a postcolonial debate raised on the soil of the European colonial project. Thus the importance of the question suggested by Mudimbe in the introduction of *The Invention of Africa*: what does it mean to be an African and philosopher today, that is, after the experience of colonization? Many phenomena upon which an African thinker can elaborate are for the most part "not only unthinkable outside of a space circumscribed by African elements but also well determined by anthropology and the colonial saga, as well as the practices and missionizing of Islam and Christianity."[32] These practices as well as anthropological and the colonial saga are defined by traditions that must be considered when speaking of African philosopher or philosophy.

THINKING FROM TRADITIONS AND PLACES HISTORICALLY AND GEOPOLITICALLY CONSTRUCTED

In his commentaries on the principle of identity, Heidegger formulated one old and provocative lesson: "Whatever and however we may try to think, we think within the sphere of tradition. Tradition prevails when it frees us from thinking back to thinking forward, which is no longer planning. Only when we turn thoughtfully toward what has already been thought, will we be turned to use for what must still be thought."[33] In the same vein, in fact, postcolonial subjects always think from a geohistorically constructed place and from many traditions. And the articulation of our discourse reveals how we inhabit these places and traditions, if it is not them that inhabit or dominate us. We can inhabit these places and traditions, live or relate to them as servants, as temple guards or as creative subjects that transforms them according to our needs. In this sense, instead of starting from influences or legacies to determine the alleged authenticity of a thinker who happens to originate from Africa, we could instead focus on examining the ways he uses the African traditions and the Western philosophical or literary tradition encountered during his education. Is he an illustrator or rather, does he use them as material or a toolbox in the service of his philosophical or literary project? In this last case, we would therefore see which of the Western philosophical tradition's leading figures are exploited and for what purpose and which elements of a foreign philosophy are internalized and used by African philosophers. Indeed just as a thinker such as Saint Augustine can be represented according to different historical periods with their own challenges—medieval Augustine is probably not the same as that of the Enlightenment—, in the same sense, there can be an American Derrida who is not exactly the French Derrida and an African Derrida who is not quite the American or French one. What matters here is how Derrida is inscribed in the debate or the discourse of African philosophers facing the situation of human existence in the postcolonial African condition. It would be interesting to see how Derrida's work on orality is received or amplified by African philosophers whose tradition have been identified as oral, in opposition to European civilization. As we can see, place thus becomes determinative, but it is not understood as simple and banal empirical evidence. Nor is it reduced to geographical space as Houtondji proposed, in order to position Guillaume Antoine Amo as an African philosopher, thus modifying the definition of African philosophy and escaping a mythological Africanity.[34] While supporting the need to reject the mythological conception of Africanity, our concept of place resembles that of V.Y. Mudimbe who, responding to those who reproached him for racializing science, states:

> Racialization? Not really. I start from the fact that my conscience and my effort are from a given place, space and moment; and I do not see how or why my speech, whatever its take off may be (*quel que soit son envol*), should not, above all else, be the cry and the witness of this singular place. Thus, it is for us to promote this important norm: a reflection on ourselves (*un arrêt sur nous-mêmes*), or more precisely, a constant return on what we are with particular fervour and attention given to our archaeological milieu; a milieu that, if it allows our *prises de parole*, also explains them.[35]

What is interesting here is that specificity or the particular is not opposed to the universal, at least if one conceives of the latter in the manner of Césaire. In fact, for Césaire, the universal is indeed "rich with the particular, rich with all particulars, the deepening and coexistence of all particulars."[36] We are also close to the geopolitics of knowledge as suggested by the opening words of Argentine philosopher Enrique Dussel's *Philosophy of Liberation*: "A philosophy of liberation must always begin by presenting the historico-ideological genesis of what it attempts to think through, giving priority to its spatial, worldly setting."[37] Convinced that abstract and non-conflictual spaces are naive and unreal, Dussel, on behalf of a philosophical realism, decided "to take space, geopolitical space, seriously." He wanted to take the following truth more seriously and use it as the starting point of his project for a philosophy of liberation: "To be born at the North Pole or in Chiapas is not the same thing as to be born in New York City."[38] To further extend Dussel's thinking, one could say: "To philosophize from the South is not exactly the same thing as to philosophize from the North."

By referring to Dussel and the geopolitics of knowledge, we seek to highlight two important things. First, accentuating the relationship between place—as it is constituted historically and geographically—and thought, is a way to emphasize the fact that "knowledge is not something produced from a postmodern non-place. On the contrary, knowledge is always geo-historically and geo-politically located."[39] Secondly, the philosophy of liberation draws its energy and *raison d'être* from a concrete place. Contrary to Hountondji's approach, Chiapas is not reduced to a simple geographical concept but is understood as a "metaphor for humanity suffering under the yoke of global capitalism."[40] It is from such a localization of the thinking process that one can understand the relation of Dussel or Mudimbe to Michel Foucault or other eurocentric critics of modernity:

> Michel Foucault, especially in his masterful *Archeology of Knowledge* . . . can help us, for instance, as a way, as a method to "retrace" the history of the "developmentalist" fallacy, present still in him and all of modern philosophy, and in order to describe the origin of our peripheral consciousness as a "fissure" of Exteriority . . . The same can be said of the attempts of Jacques Derrida, Jean-François Lyotard, or Gianni Vattimo. Like Friedrich Nietzsche, they help us as "destroyers," but little as "reconstructors."[41]

One can remember that in *The Invention of Africa*, Mudimbe states that "despite their violence against the rule of the Same and the history of its conquests over all regionalisms, specificities, and differences, Lévi-Strauss and Foucault . . . belong to the signs of the Same power. What they represent could be considered an expression of the 'intelligence' of the Same. As Foucault himself stated, referring to his own intellectual filiation: 'Can one still philosophize where Hegel is no longer possible? Can any philosophy continue to exist that is no longer Hegelian?'."[42]

We find the same positioning in the work of Moroccan thinker Abdelkebir Khatibi involved in the decolonization project of the social sciences and of the development of "An Other Thinking ('Une pensée-autre')."[43] The place from which Khatibi speaks justifies his critical relation to European critics of modernity such as Derrida, Lyotard, Foucault, Nietzsche or Heidegger. If, on the one hand, the Moroccan thinker can find allies in these critics of modernity and promoters of a thought of difference, on the other hand, the memory of the Maghreb with its rich knowledge and traditions marginalized by modern reason requires him to maintain distance with respect to Eurocentric critics of modernity. The distance maintained appears as one of the conditions for the emergence of "another thinking," taking its starting point from the subjective understanding of what Mignolo calls "the colonial wound."[44]

That said, it is important to stress that a thinker who is not of Mexican origin, but who is aware of the darker underside of modern and dominant reason, can also choose to think from the perspective of Chiapas, as Sartre attempted to do with *Black Orpheus*, Fanon with Algeria and the Spanish Jesuit Ignacio Ellacuria with El Salvador, where he became a major protagonist of the theology/philosophy of liberation. As the case of the Jesuit who opted to take Salvadorian nationality illustrates, we are in the presence of thinkers taking on a prophetic function. Using categories put back into circulation by Bourdieu, one could say that Fanon, Sartre and Ellacuria and Dussel took on the function of *auctor*, as opposed to that of *lector* (of a tradition), whom we have also called the temple guard. In fact, the mission of the *lector* is to illustrate an established tradition and to avoid any transgression or treason, in short to ensure its accurate transmission. To put it another way, the lector is a teacher. He is not expected to modify the culture. His mission is to serve the tradition, to make sure that the legacy of the past is known and transmitted." He is assigned the mission of ensuring that the sacred message is understood and that we live and speak from this tradition. Whereas the *lector* is defined by his intellectual orthodoxy, the *auctor* is characterised by his powerfully subversive intent. As Mudimbe puts it, "an auctor is a prophetic thinker exploring the margins of a social formation and interrogating a tradition and its institutions, and a lector, or a priestly figure whose role is to maintain the essence of a culture and its tradition."[45]

"LECTOR" AND "AUCTOR" IN AFRICAN PHILOSOPHY

These two functions can be used to differentiate the ways that Africans approach the Western philosophical tradition. On the one hand, those called Europhilosophers may legitimately be considered *lectores*. As Prosper Laleye explains, in their erudite commentaries, they "perpetuate the European philosophical tradition,"[46] which seems to be philosophy *par excellence*. For the latter, the African cannot, in the name of difference, afford the luxury of philosophizing as if Kant, Marx, Hegel, etc., never existed. In this way, the established philosophical tradition is a prerequisite and a guide for the African who wishes to engage in philosophical practice. However, Hountondji, who was considered to be the leader of "europhilosophers," prompts the African philosopher to avoid a servile attitude in relation to the international philosophical tradition. In short, considering philosophy as a scientific discipline with its own tradition, Hountondji provides a strategy of critical and selective appropriation of this philosophical tradition based on African concerns. The international tradition, he writes, "has meaning only when it is supported, updated, revived and thus, enriched and developed by the best of what it possesses, by African society itself."[47] Ultimately, the Beninese philosopher wants the African philosopher to be able to philosophize as a philosophical equal, that is to say liberated from all the mythologies of difference.

However, if we consider the institutionalization of philosophy in Africa and its symbolic power, Hountondji's position, while seeking the liberation of African discourse, remains somewhat ambiguous. This ambiguity is primarily related to the place accorded to the centrality of tradition in the practice of the philosophical discipline, to the point of relativizing the relationship between thought and place. One might ask, as Emmanuel Renault does at the end of *Marx et la philosophie*, should we really worry if we come "to practice philosophy in ways that have little to do with how we have understood it until now? Is it not an ambition of traditional philosophy to produce radical ruptures not only in principles and methods, but even in the idea that we have of philosophy?"[48] The answer to this question comes from the *auctor*.

The position of the *auctor* in African philosophy seems to be illustrated by the Cameroonian philosopher Fabien Eboussi Boulaga for whom precisely the place (non-abstract, concrete, always existential) in which one philosophizes plays an important role. It can induce displacement in tradition, practice, philosophical concepts and even in the function of philosophy. Thus, for example, Eboussi suggests that rather than questioning or commenting upon the major themes examined by great philosophers (*philosophia perennis*), it would be more interesting within and from the African context, to question what they have ignored (and why?), what they were powerless to clarify (and why?) or what they obscured. Eboussi Boulaga writes:

> Racism is such a limitation of many philosophical discourses. It exposes large conceptual systems as sheer and cannibalistic hoaxes. Others claim to be apolitical while partaking of the will to power inscribed in the imperial, avid, and exclusive conception of truth in the monopoly of knowledge that confirms the others' inhumanity and is absolved from any duty or guilt by the absolute detachment of understanding or of being qua being. Race and power point to other locations from which thinking could start. They suggest that the human will think what there is only by retaking a position in one's most concrete, historical and diverse being.[49]

Eboussi Boulaga thus refuses any "traditionalization" of philosophy, that is reducing philosophy to an authoritarian tradition, to repeat or to reproduce, because this closes the door to creativity: "creation is forbidden, as it would mean looking for legitimacy beyond the existing power system, as it might unleash and bring back what has been repressed and therewith other experts and other 'elites'."[50] For Eboussi Boulaga, "To acquiesce in the traditionalization of philosophy, in the obligation to think through the interposition and mediation of philosophical ancestry, is to ratify an ethnocentrism that manifests its destructiveness and homicidal potential when transposed in other areas."[51] To which he adds: "The ignorance of such implications takes place in the new configuration of the balance of forces, which were fully perceived previously and rejected by those who, in reaction, strove toward securing a 'philosophical tradition of their own'."[52]

These remarks bring us closer to an important principle of Eboussi Boulaga's philosophical practice that Silvia Riva captures in the Foucauldian expression of "differential topology."[53] This demonstrates the importance of the concrete and existential place from which the philosophical act is carried out. Echoing Dussel who asserts that thinking from the North (London or New York, for example) is not the same thing as thinking from the South (Chiapas, or Soweto for example), Eboussi Boulaga suggests that when the Muntu speaks or expresses himself, he does so from a different place than that assigned to him in a closed system. A new topography is established which can lead to a displacement of concepts, another manner of questioning and the assignment of a different function to philosophy. In other words, when a new topography emerges,

> "Philosophy" enters unexpected configurations and constellations. This results in other questions, standpoints, as well as new associations and interests. Under the cover of the same words and practices, diverging objects are pursued; perhaps more accurately, philosophy is caused to play new roles and undergo a functional transformation. Instead of endless commentaries on its canon, with restoration of its antiquated functions in order to "adapt" them, its object is deconstructed by setting it in motion. To have "philosophy" move from one place to another and strike up strange connections is, if not inventing or recreating it, at least bestowing other statuses and usages upon it. Alteration may yield inconsistent medleys and decay. If it is deliberative and well considered, it becomes expressive of a want in being to be satisfied and a march toward lucidity and authenticity.[54]

It is also in this sense that instead of the professional philosopher who, immune to events, "engages in the game of the aesthete and the erudite," Eboussi Boulaga prefers the individual who is compelled by the events he endured "to write as he shouts or cries."[55] This is the signature of a thinker for whom the criteria of a philosophical discourse are not given or found in virtue of a general methodology or epistemology capable of defining philosophy in a stipulative or apodictic way. They are the clarification of immanent logic of a chosen way of life that asserts itself and confronts the problems of its constitutive structure, of its operation and of its exchanges or interactions with the surrounding world. In fact, for

Eboussi Boulaga, philosophy is not a theory of a scientific practice, but first and foremost "a way of life . . . a manner to behave with regard to the realities symbolized or captioned by words such as 'reality,' 'the real' and 'being',"[56] in short, a way of answering the question: how should we live? Or better yet: what is a good life?

It is in the space between the positions of *lector* and *auctor* that the generation of young African philosophers who entered the field in the late '80s seem to position themselves. For this postcolonial generation, the question of the place of the Western philosophical tradition in African philosophical practice arose in a pragmatic fashion. Refusing all fixity of identity and all mythology of exclusive difference, African philosophy becomes of more and more a "movement," a "meeting place" and a "crossing (*une traversée*)."[57] But like Eboussi Boulaga, young African philosophers continue to pay attention to the limits of Western philosophies when they are transposed to other contexts. Séverine Kodjo-Grandvaux rightly resorted to the image of *détour* to discuss the use of Western philosophies in the contemporary African philosophical practice. Through the African philosophical practice, she writes, we see "how each time the themes developed by African philosophers are, in a way, the opportunity to divert from Western philosophies"[58] or to show their limits.[59] In other words, African philosophy reveals what happens to the philosophies of dominant Western tradition when they are examined or mobilized in other contexts and traditions. Evidently, the *mot d'ordre* is not fidelity to philosophies already philosophized, as Laleye would say, but creativity depending on the location, the experience or the context. Some recent titles by young authors like Mbimbi Mbamba,[60] Bidima,[61] and Kabisa Bular[62] bear witness to this process. But *Hegel et la philosophie africaine. Une lecture interprétative de la dialectique hégélienne* (*Hegel and African Philosophy. An interpretative reading of the Hegelian dialectic*) by Médéwale-Jacob Agossou[63] seems to be one of the best examples. As his title may suggest, Agossou seeks to answer the following question: what is reading Hegel from Africa in general, and how can the African reader benefit from reading him? His work validates the approach that takes into consideration the place from which we speak and from which we read. One could say that these works are explicitly or implicitly crafted on Eboussi-Boulaga's question which echoes the criticism of Laleye: "How to read philosophy without using it as an excuse to run away from one's condition and elude the questions posed by our concrete situation?."[64] Or: " how to take up again and to reutilize the philosophic discipline in such a way as to be concerned by it, so that it remains, becomes or is restored as a practice over being human, of a free being"?[65] In short, the philosophical tradition is reduced to the role of channel that supports new philosophical methods. We can borrow from Janz's explaining what he called "philosophy-in-place" to summarize the approach of young contemporary philosophers:

> Philosophy-in-place is more than the philosophical analysis of the concept of place. . . . It is the realization that we always stand on shifting ground as we philosophize, that we are always implicated by the concepts we use, and that they never remain stable. We add to interpretive possibilities of concepts, the provenance, as we use them, and this accumulation is more than just accretion. Furthermore, the concepts that we analyze as philosophers frequently travel across discursive boundaries, whether they be disciplinary or cultural, and that travel means that a concept will always get used metaphorically.[66]

For Janz, this means that "we must engage with the direct meaning of concepts, their provenance, and at the same time allow the concepts to raise our own place to question." Ultimately, the process makes possible "open-ended creation of new concepts, ones which make universals available (that is, allow us to recognize and built on connections across cultural, disciplinary, and other boundaries), and also clarifies and establishes one's own identity."[67]

African philosophers of the first generation used this strategic principle of diversion (*détour*) in their proper manner. With regards to this generation, Mudimbe has clearly demonstrated that it was not by chance that between 1955 and 1970, the work of Africans focused mainly on those he calls "really 'compromising' European thinkers." That is to say, European thinkers who were questioning the Western philosophical tradition and were searching for other ways forward or for a renewal of philosophy to escape positivism, the domination of technological reason or the forgetting of Being (Heidegger). Thus, for example, "Elungu Pene Elungu specialized in Malebranche's philosophy; Hountondji chose Husserl and Comte; Senghor commented upon Teilhard de Chardin's theses; Towa was then working on Hegel; Ngindu beginning his book on Laberthonnière, and Ugirashebuja completing his research on Heidegger."[68]

Octave Ugirashebuja's concluding remarks in his study on Heidegger speak for themselves. At the end of his book, commenting on Heidegger's assertions according to which the poet "prepares the poetic, is the background upon which humanity, provided it has a history, makes its home," the Rwandan philosopher writes:

> This speech is to be understood, it seems, in the sense that Heidegger spoke of the work of art as historial determination. All artistic creation, every birth of a poem is the 'Advent of Being.' It is the beginning of a new time, because real time is that of Being or the implementation of truth. This manifestation of Being is in the work of art, it takes place in a given people. It thus makes the true history of this people.[69]

Following this comment are two short, but crucial paragraphs, which not only allow us to further perceive what is at stake in the author's thesis, but also locates the work within debates amongst African philosophers:

> Yet, all people are capable of artistic creation, all people are poetic in the sudden appearance of their language. We just need (O slow maturation!) there to be thinkers who listen to this language and poets who ensure that the essential words do not become pure communication signals.
>
> It seems to me that Heidegger invites us all, Africans, Westerners and Easterners to this listening of Being in the song in the language which is ours, in the poetry of our poets and in the art of our artists. For it is there that Being manifests itself and gives way for man to learn to live as a man rather than as a rational animal.[70]

Indeed, as Mudimbe notes, the author discussed or commented upon serves as a mirror. "One notes a remarkable mediation between the rigor of a philosophical exercise and the fantasies of a political insurrection: the text commented upon is a mirror which reveals the self to the reader or commentator."[71] He actually goes further. Commenting on the work of Ugirashebuja, he writes:

> At any rate, our contemporary students of *philosophia perennis* may also be troubling. One is surely taken aback when, in examining these very classical analyses, one comes across presuppositions on African otherness in the guise of logical deduction. For example, it is a surprise to follow Ugirashebuja discovering in Heidegger'writing Banyarwanda's language as a sign of being and its nomination, and to discover in the Rwandese philosopher's text the voice of Heidegger inviting all of us—Westernes, Africans, Asians—to listen to being in our respective languages.[72]

But is the European tradition only a mirror, as Mudimbe suggests? What these philosophers in African condition are doing is it only an "amplification" of the European tradition? If we follow Ugirashebuja's reading closely, we can see that the Western author, in this case Heidegger, ultimately becomes a pretext, which leads to another cause: the possibility of an African philosophy that is rooted in the languages and the artistic creations of the African people. In other words, in the name of the same methodological principles, Africans seek or aim for something else. The place that Heidegger grants to language and poetry signifies not only the possibility to develop an African philosophy from language, poetry and works of art of the African people but the possibility of another philosophical tradition that can enter into dialogue with the Western tradition which would thus be reduced to the status of one tradition amongst others. Here we have a sense of the importance of a project, which would consist in reading African readings of the Western philosophical tradition and examining the various facets this tradition takes in the African philosophical tradition. We could thus see what dimension of Derrida's, Kant's, Sartre's, Foucault's or Habermas' philosophy became African, that is to say are inscribed in the development of the African tradition, a tradition thereby representing itself as an open place or *un espace métissé*.

The African place from which the question of philosophy arises is a place from which lines of flight can be traced. This implies a complex dialectic in which the movement of territorialization is "opposed by a corresponding, simultaneous movement of deterritorialization: an outwardly-turning movement that breaks up territorial boundaries," and vice versa.[73] Due to this complex dialectic, a European philosopher can become an African philosopher. And in Derrida's case, the African philosopher can become European philosopher, that is, an African who thinks from Western tradition of philosophy. All this as the ghost of Amo haunts us, some three centuries later, reminding us that, when it comes to thinking, there is no such thing as determinism of origins.

NOTES

1. V.Y. Mudimbe, *The Invention of Africa. Gnosis, Philosophy and the Order of Knowledge*, (Indianapolis: Indiana University Press, 1988).
2. Bruce Janz, *Philosophy in an African Place*, (Boulder, New York: Lexington Books, 2009).
3. Gilles Deleuze and Félix Guattari, *What Is Philosophy?* Trans. Hugh Tomlinson and Graham Burchell (New York: Columbia University Press, 1996), 85.
4. Jacques Derrida, "Of Humanities and the Philosophical Discipline: The Right to Philosophy from the Cosmopolitical Point of View (the Example of an International Institution), " *Surfaces* IV, 310 Folio1 (1994)
5. Bruce Janz, *Philosophy in a African Place*, 2.
6. Gilles Deleuze and Félix Guattari, *What Is Philosophy* ?, 85.
7. Roberto Esposito, *Living Thought. The Origins and Actuality of Italian Philosophy*, trans. Zakiya Hanafi (Stanford, CA: Stanford University Press, 2012), 13.
8. Janz, *Philosophy in an African Place*, 6.
9. *Ibid.*
10. Paulin Hountondji, *African Philosophy, Myth and Reality*, (Bloomington: Indiana University Press, 1983), 33.
11. *Ibid.*, 112.
12. *Ibid.*, 129.
13. Kwame Anthony Appiah, *The Lies that Bind. Rethinking Identity* , (London: Profile Books Ltd, 2018), 110.
14. *Ibid.*
15. Shamil Jeppie and Souleymane Bachir Diagne, *The Meaning of Timbuktu*, (Cape Town: CODESRIA/HSRS, 2008).
16. Paulin Hountondji, *African Philosophy, Myth and Reality*, 129.
17. *Ibid.*
18. *Ibid.*, 129-130.
19. V.Y. Mudimbe, *Parables & Fables. Exegesis, Textuality , and Politics in Central Africa*, (Madison: The University of Wisconsin Press, 1991), 7.
20. *Ibid.*, 14.
21. V.Y. Mudimbe, *Tales of Faith. Religion as Political Performance in Central Africa*, (London & Atlantic Highlands, NJ: The Athlone Press, 1997), 198-199.
22. Paul Gilroy, *Between Camps. Nations, Cultures and the Allure of Race*, (New York: Routledge, 2004).
23. Reinhart Koselleck, Reinhart, *Enlightenment and the Pathogenesis of Modern Society*. Boston: MIT Press, 1988.
24. V.Y. Mudimbe, *The Invention of Africa, 83*.
25. *Ibid.*, 84.

26. V.Y. Mudimbe, *L'odeur du Père. Essais sur des limites de la science et de la vie en Afrique noire*, (Paris: Présence africaine, 1982), 138-139.
27. V.Y. Mudimbe, *The Invention of Africa*, 85.
28. Georges Balandier, *Sociologie des Brazzavilles noirs*, (Paris : Aramand Colin, 1955).
29. V.Y. Mudimbe, *The Invention of Africa*, 86.
30. Roberto Esposito, *Living Thought*, 12.
31. Michel Hauser, *Essai sur la poétique de la négritude*, (Paris, Silex, 1986).
32. V.Y. Mudimbe, *Tales of Faith*, 198.
33. Martin Heidegger, *Identity and Difference*, (New York: Harper and Row, 1969), 41.
34. Paulin Hountondji, *African Philosophy, Myth and Reality*, 66.
35. V.Y. Mudimbe, *L'odeur du père*, 14.
36. Ibid.
37. Enrique Dussel, *Philosophy of Liberation*, (Maryknoll (N.Y.) : Orbis Books, 1985), 1.
38. Ibid., 2.
39. Walter Mignolo, *The Idea of Latin America*, (Malden (MA): Blackwell Publishing, 2005), 43.
40. Ibid., 66.
41. Enrique Dussel, *The Underside of Modernity Appel, Ricoeur, Taylor and the Philosophy of Liberation*, (New Jersey: Humanities Press, 1996), 4.
42. V.Y. Mudimbe, *The Invention of Africa*, 43.
43. Abdelkebir Khatibi, *Maghreb pluriel*, (Paris: Denoël, 1983).
44. Walter Mignolo, *The Idea of Latin America*, 120.
45. V.Y. Mudimbe, *Tales of Faith*, 175.
46. Issiaka Prosper Laleye, "L'élan du philosopher face à l'ordre comme norme sociale. Dialectique des droits et des devoirs du philosophe aujourd'hui," in *Actes de la 9e semaine Philosophique de Kinshasa*, (Kinshasa: Facultés Catholiques de Kinshasa, 1985), 32.
47. Paulin Hountondji, "Que peut la philosophie?," *Présence Africaine 119* (1981), 69.
48. Emmanuel Renault, *Marx et la philosophie*, (Paris : PUF, 3013), 201.
49. Fabien Eboussi Boulaga, *Muntu in Crisis. African Authenticity and Philosophy*, (Trenton (N.J): Africa World Press, 2014), 127.
50. Eboussi Boulaga, *Muntu in Crisis*, 86-87.
51. Ibid., 89.
52. Ibid.
53. Silvia Riva, "Pour une 'topologie différentielle.' Le diagnostic du présent dans la pensée de Fabien Eboussi Boulaga," in Lidia Procesi and Kasereka Kavwahirehi eds. *Beyond the Lines : Fabien Eboussi Boulaga, a Philosophical Practice*, (Munich (Germany) : Lincom Europa, 2012), 209–227.
54. Fabien Eboussi Boulaga, *Muntu in Crisis*, 124-125.
55. Ibid., 246.
56. Ibid., 186.
57. Severine Kodjo-Gravaux, *Philosophies africaines*, (Paris: *Présence Africaine*, 2013), 189.
58. Severine Kodjo –Gravaux, *Philosophies africaines*, 172.
59. Gervais Yamb, *Droits humains, Démocratie, État de droit: John Rawls, Habermas et Eboussi Boulaga*, (Paris: L'Harmattan, 2009).
60. Mbimbi Mbamba *La phénoménologie de la religion du jeune Heidegger et sa signification pour la théologie : contribution à la critique de la religiosité africaine*, (Frankfurt: PIE Peter Lang, 2012).
61. Jean-Godefroy Bidima, *Théorie critique et modernité négro-africaine: de l'école de Francfort à la docta spes africana*, (Paris: Publications de la Sorbonne, 1993).
62. Jean-Baptiste Kabisa Bular, *Singularité des traditions et universalisme de la Démocratie. Étude critique inspirée d'Eric Weil*, (Paris : L'Harmattan, 2007).

63. Médéwalé-Jacob, Agossou, *Hegel et la philosophie africaine. Une lecture interprétative de la dialectique hégélienne*, (Paris: Karthala), 2005.
64. Fabien Eboussi Boulaga, *Muntu in Crisis*, 185.
65. Ibid., 205.
66. Bruce Janz, *Philosophy in an African Place*, 12
67. Ibid.
68. V.Y. Mudimbe, *The Invention of Africa*, 43.
69. Octave Ugirashebuja, *Dialogue entre la pensée et la poésie d'après Heidegger*, (Bruxelles: Lumen Vitae, 1977), 227.
70. Ibid.
71. Mudimbe, *The Invention of Africa*, 42-43.
72. Ibid, 162.
73. Esposito, *Living Thought*, 13.

WORKS CITED

Agossou, M-J. *Hegel et la philosophie africaine. Une lecture interprétative de la dialectique hégélienne*. Paris: Karthala, 2005.
Appiah, Kwame Anthony. *The Lies that Bind. Rethinking Identity*. London: Profile Books Ltd, 2018.
Balandier, G. *Sociologie actuelle de l'Afrique noire*. Paris: Presses universitaires de France, 1955.
———. *Sociologie des Brazzavilles noirs*. Paris: Armand Colin, 1955.
Bidima, J. G. *Théorie critique et modernité négro-africaine: de l'école de Francfort à la docta spes africana*. Paris: Publications de la Sorbonne, 1993.
Deleuze, Gilles and Guattari, Felix. *What is Philosophy?* Trans. Hugh Tomlinson and Graham Burchell. New York: Columbia University Press, 1996.
Derrida, Jacques. "Of Humanities and the Philosophical Disciplines: The Right to Philosophy from the Cosmopolitical Point of View (the Example of an International Institution), " *Surfaces* IV, 310 Folio1 (1994), Montréal. www.pum.umontreal.ca/revues/surfaces/vol4/derrida.html (May 2018).
Diagne, Souleymane Bachir. *L'Encre des savants. Réflexions sur la philosophie en Afrique*. Paris: Présence africaine/Codesria, 2013.
Dussel, Enrique. *Philosophy of Liberation*, Maryknoll (N.Y.) : Orbis Books, 1985.
———. *The Underside of Modernity Appel, Ricoeur, Taylor and the Philosophy of Liberation*. New Jersey: Humanities Press, 1996.
Eboussi Boulaga, Fabien. *L'Affaire de la philosophie africaine. Au-delà des querelles*. Paris: Karthala, 2011.
———. *Muntu in Crisis. African Authenticity and Philosophy*. Trenton (N.J): Africa World Press, 2014.
Esposito, Roberto. *Living Thought. The Origins and Actuality of Italian Philosophy*, trans. Zakiya Hanafi. Stanford, CA: Stanford University Press, 2012.
Gilroy, Paul. *Between Camps, Nations, Cultures and the Allure of Race*. New York: Routledge, 2004.
Heidegger, Martin. *Identity and Difference*. New York: Harper and Row, 1969.
Hountondji, P. *African Philosophy, Myth and Reality*. Bloomington: Indiana University Press, 1983.
———. "Que peut la philosophie?," *Présence Africaine* 119 (1981): 47-71.
Janz, Bruce B. *Philosophy in an African Place*. Lanham, Boulder, New York: Lexington Books, 2009.
Jeppie, Shamil and Diagne, Souleymane B. eds. The Meaning of Timbuktu. Cape Town: CODESRIA/HSRS Press, 2008.
Kabisa Bular, J-B. *Singularité des traditions et universalisme de la Démocratie. Étude critique inspire d'Eric Weil*. Paris: L'harmattan, 2007.
Khatibi, Abdelkebir. *Maghreb pluriel*. Paris: Denoël, 1983.

Kodjo-Grandvaux, Séverine. *Philosophies africaines*. Paris: *Présence africaine*, 2013.
Koselleck, Reinhart, *Enlightenment and the Pathogenesis of Modern Society*. Boston: MIT Press, 1988.
Laleye, Issiaka-Prosper. "L'élan du philosopher face à l'ordre comme norme sociale. Dialectiques des droits et des devoirs du philosophe africain, " in *Actes de la 9 ^{e} Semaine Philosophique de Kinshasa*. Kinshasa : Faculté Catholique de Kinshasa, 1985 : 19-35.
Mbimbi Mbamba, J-C. *La phénoménologie de la religion du jeune Heidegger et sa signification pour la théologie : contribution à la critique de la religiosité africaine*. Frankfurt: PIE Peter Lang, 2012.
Mignolo, Walter D. "The Geopolitics of Knowledge and the Colonial Difference," in *The South Atlantic Quaterly* 101 (2002): 57–96.
———. *The Idea of Latin America*. Malden (MA): Blackwell Publishing, 2005.
Mudimbe, V.Y. *The Invention of Africa. Gnosis, Philosophy and the Order of Knowledge*. Bloomington: Indiana University Press, 1988.
———. *L'odeur du Père. Essais sur des limites de la science et de la vie en Afrique noire*. Paris: Présence africaine, 1982.
———. *Parables & Fables. Exegesis, Textuality , and Politics in Central Africa*. Madison: The University of Wisconsin Press, 1991.
———. *Tales of Faith. Religion as Political Performance in Central Africa*. London &Atlantic Highlands, NJ : The Athlone Press, 1997.
Renault, Emmanuel. *Marx et la philosophie*. Paris : PUF, 2013.
Riva, Silvia. "Pour une 'topologie différentielle.' Le diagnostic du présent dans la pensée de Fabien Eboussi Boulaga." In Lidia Procesi and Kasereka Kavwahirehi eds. *Beyond the Lines : Fabien Eboussi Boulaga, a Philosophical Practice*. Munich (Germany) : Lincom Europa, 2012 : 209–227.
Ugirashebuja, Octave. *Dialogue entre la pensée et la poésie d'après Heidegger*. Bruxelles: Lumen Vitae, 1977.
Yamb, G.-D. *Droits humains, Démocratie, État de droit: John Rawls, Habermas et Eboussi Boulaga*. Paris: L'Harmattan, 2009.

Afterword

Respect for Derrida and Africa

Jean-Paul Martinon

One of the most striking features of this collection of chapters is the respect that the authors have for their topic: Derrida and Africa. Amidst all the predictable unsettledness, the requisite out-of-jointness, the compulsory a-contemporaneity and out-of-placeness, the obligatory haunting that is always no-longer and/or not-yet, the mandatory and never finished mourning, amidst all these telltale signs of good Derridean thinking, one thing curiously remains steadfast and unchanging: respect. Respect for the man who lived between 1930 and 2004, for a continent named Africa, for the dual topic under scrutiny, and for the scholarship that gives rise to all these thoughts about Derrida and Africa. At no point in this collection is there a sudden disrespect for Derrida or Africa, a way of contemptuously saying "no" to the man who wrote so much or the continent that gives so much. Not that one would expect a lack of civility or ungraciousness, but one might expect, at least, that one of these scholars rejects both the man who once lived in Paris and/or this continent of over a billion people. But each contributor respectfully says "yes" to both. As such, respect permeates every thought here, even when these thoughts veer off the topic at hand.

Now, how is one to make sense of this formidably unfaltering respect that seems to contrast so blatantly with the prerequisite undecidedness that always pervades writings inspired by Derrida? To answer this question, I will first go back to Derrida's own interpretation of this respect. How does Derrida understand respect? In the limited context of an Afterword, I can only limit myself to one reading amidst all of his oeuvre and scholarship: his reading of Emmanuel Levinas's understanding of respect. How does Derrida, through Levinas, makes sense of respect? This will constitute the first part of this Afterword. I will then see how the scholars invited to contribute to this collection of chapters on the topic of Derrida and Africa are true to this Derridean form of respect. The aim is obviously not to reveal these scholars' respectful attitudes (or lack of), but to uncover what overall sustains itself as a permanent ethical fixture in any form of deconstructive writing, especially when this writing concerns Africa.

There is obviously no space to retrace here the way Derrida formulates, following Levinas, his own understanding of the issue of respect *in its entirety*. One would have to re-read carefully the many instances when Derrida interacts not only with Levinas's thought, but also with that of his closest contemporaries, Buber, Bataille, Heidegger, or Blanchot, to name only a few. The only thing one can do in the limited space of this Afterword is to read a crucial few passages from "Violence and Metaphysics" in which Derrida directly addresses the problems of Levinas's attempt to come up with a philosophy of respect. He writes:

> In the last analysis, according to Levinas, [the] language [of respect] would be a language which would do without the verb *to be*, that is, without predication. Predication is the first violence. Since the verb *to be* and the predicative act are implied in every other verb, and in every common noun, [the] language [of respect], in the last analysis, would be a language of pure invocation, pure adoration, proffering only proper nouns in order to call to the other from afar. In effect, such a language would be purified of all rhetoric, which is what Levinas explicitly desires; and purified of the first sense of rhetoric, which we can invoke without artifice, that is, purified of every *verb*. Would such a language still deserve its name? Is a language free from all rhetoric possible? The Greeks, who taught us what *Logos* meant, would never have accepted this. Plato tells us in the *Cratylus* (425a), the *Sophist* (262 ad) and in *Letter VII* (342b), that there is no Logos which does not suppose the interlacing of nouns and verbs.[1]

Let us play, for a moment, devil's advocate: if one is seriously going to follow Levinas, then one needs to accept the fact that respect can only occur if a language of invocation is used, that is, if a "pure" language—without predication or the verb "to be"—is put forward. "I (invocation) you, I (adoration) you." These are the only ways respect can take place. The "I" and the "you" of these sentences do not even amount to the recognition of a subject or ego and the invocation or adoration here does not even manage to be an active and therefore aggressive appropriation of the other. I don't write "I invoke you, I adore you." I bracket the invocation and adoration in order to avoid at all costs the violence of verbs. Not unlike the unpronounceable YHWH, "you" remain therefore a subject of total invocation and adoration: untouched, unobjectified, and therefore, unharmed. This is the only end to Levinas's pious language; a language that never violates the other, that never becomes Greek, that is, a "dirty" language full of authoritative predicative sentences that violate the other.

But is this reasonable? Can one really remain purely in the realm of invocation or adoration, that is, a language devoid of verbs? Are we not always already in a world of contamination, half-Jew-half-Greek? Is it not

Levinas himself who teaches us elsewhere (paradoxically) that there is no escaping the realm of violence and therefore the realm of war? And if this is the case, should we then abandon all Levinasean forms of invocation or adoration and therefore all genuine attempts to truthfully respect the other? As the quotation above makes clear, Derrida's answer is a resounding: "Yes!" Let's abandon Levinas's verb-less attempt to be respectful, let's simply try to reduce the violence of Logos as much as possible, knowing that a Logos free of violence is ultimately impossible. With such an unambiguous affirmation, verbs must therefore be restrained of their violent ways. But how is one to reduce the violence of predicative sentences? How does this Derridean respect that always already remains in the realm of war manifests itself without, in the end, violating the other? How does Derrida understand respect *after* Levinas?

In order to make sense of Derrida's own take on the issue of respect, I would like to simply explore a key concept in Derrida's work discretely exposed in "Violence and Metaphysics": the verb "to ac-knowledge." With such a quick foray into Derrida's own understanding of this expression, I will then be able to return to the preceding essays with a much clearer idea of how they maintain a form of respect for their topic (Derrida and Africa) and the authors they involve.

In a section of "Violence and Metaphysics," entitled "Ontological Violence," Derrida puts forward three verbs to make sense of respect: "to pre-comprehend," "to com-prehend" and "to ac-knowledge."[2] In each case, the verb is always left open with a hyphen. There is unfortunately, no space here to make sense of this differentiation, especially with regards to the French: *pre-comprendre, com-prendre,* and *re-connaitre*. I will focus here exclusively, for lack of space, on the last verb ("to ac-knowledge") while keeping the other two in mind. So let me first see how one can understand this differentiation that Derrida makes between the verb open with a hyphen ("to ac-knowledge") and the verb left unhyphenated ("to acknowledge")? Such a seemingly pointy and perhaps, to some, pedantic focus should reveal a great deal about Derrida and respect.

Firstly, "to acknowledge," in one word, usually refers to the acceptance of the truth or existence of something or someone: "I acknowledge this table in front of me." As such, the verb "to acknowledge" serves as a possible basis for the science of epistemology insofar as it is concerned with the identification, classification, and use of knowledge. The second, "to ac-knowledge," this time opened with a hyphen, refers to an epistemic process that curiously never manages to constitute itself into a body of knowledge. Derrida's French brings together the prefix *re-* and the verb *connaitre*. Spacing out the prefix from the verb leaves in suspense the moment when knowledge stabilizes itself as something recognizable and repeatable. Similarly, the English brings together the prefix *ac-* and the noun *knowledge* (with a parasitic c mysteriously slipped in over time). Whether in French or English, this spacing out between prefix and verb or noun is therefore an attempt to think the *flight* of knowledge, its occurrence, before any form of assurance or security with regards to the knowledge gained or acquired.

As such, "I ac-knowledge" (open) achieves effectively no knowledge. It stands for an approach that withholds the possibility of any form of figuring or picturing; leaving whatever or whoever is approached most simply, un-acknowledged and therefore strictly un-identifiable, un-classifiable, and ultimately, outside of all types of taxonomies. For example, "I ac-knowledge that you are probably reading this essay and yet I cannot place you, I cannot acknowledge (one word) you properly, that is, with a name, a history, a time, and a place." Derrida's split verb is therefore an attempt to not appropriate the other, to let him be un-interpreted, un-classified, un-gendered, in a word, un-violated. The importance of the hyphen cannot be underestimated for it points to the fact that knowledge remains open; it is neither a recognition nor a cognition, which would fossilize the other, but a gesture that leaves whoever is being addressed unaffected, that is, untouched. Ultimately, the aim behind this openness is to prevent the cancelling out of the future, whereby the object of knowledge is already singled out, fixed, branded, categorized, classified and therefore subjected, controlled, mastered, and dominated. "To ac-knowledge" is to guarantee that the future can still take place.

The crucial lesson that comes out of this distinction between verbal formations (one closed, the other open) is that it opens up the possibility of conceiving how we might *begin* to formulate a language of respect. Derrida refers to this possibility with much more precision when, in his reading of Levinas, he points to the ethical way in which thought takes place. He writes: "Thought . . . conditions the *respect* for the other *as what it is*: other."[3] Derrida's move from "to ac-knowledge" to "thought" is self-evident in as much as the gesture "to ac-knowledge" can already be identified in how thought takes place. Thought indeed never settles. Thought allows us to approach the other without determination. It is precisely what leaves the other "be" always already other to me. The language of respect therefore starts not by fixing ideas concretely once and for all, but by letting thought run a course that has no pre-determined end in sight. A true language of respect can therefore only mimic the errancy of thought without at the same time being simply a divagation, prayer, or invocation.

How is one to understand this further? Derrida's short sentence contains a crucial verb that should come across as the exact opposite of any form of respect: "to condition." Thought *conditions* and this conditioning ends up paradoxically being respectful of the other. How is one to make sense of this? The conditioning here is not a way of influencing the other, but a way of fixing their irreducible alterity, that is, this alterity that, in the other, can never be identified, secured, or fossilized. In other words, however much in thought, I want to acknowledge the other, I want to appropriate the other as mine, he, she, or they remain(s) always beyond my grasp, *always conditioned as being beyond reach*. Thought effectively provides us with a conditioning process, that is, a gradual fixing that, strangely, but most clearly, secures the respect of the other; a paradoxical fact that should indeed leave all those who advocate "the respect for all" if not baffled or disconcerted, at least a little worried because, technically, it stands for the exact opposite to all traditional forms of respect whereby the other should always be left *un*conditioned.

But how is one to conceive this *conditioning* of thought that secures the alterity of the other? In order to answer this question, it is necessary to realize that, for Derrida, this conditioning is necessarily understood paradoxically both passively *and* actively. This movement of thought that never makes it as knowledge is a movement whose aim is basically to always bring forth new thoughts, that is, new horizons, new mysteries. This "bringing forth of new thoughts" is both at once active and passive. For example, "I, again, ac-knowledge you future reader." This ac-knowledgment implies an *act* that *actively* projects you into the future as a reader of *Derrida and Africa*. But this ac-knowledgment is also essentially *passive* as I am unable to know in advance who you are and what your thoughts are about Derrida and Africa. This passivity is effectively irreducible because I can never determine in advance what you will potentially think of this collection of chapters. Consequently, the activity/passivity of this ac-knowledgment is not something that can be determined in advance or judged *as* it takes place. The conditioning of respect is a way of *working actively/passively with* what can never be appropriated or judged.

So here we are. This is how respect works for Derrida, at least at the time of his reading of Levinas: it is the ac-knowledgment that there is always a movement toward the other, a movement that never accomplishes itself, thus leaving the other unaffected, untouched, unharmed, a radical alterity *conditioned*, but never guaranteed. Because "to ac-knowledge" can *only* orient itself toward the other, that is, toward a renewed mystery, it has no choice but to lean toward respect, that is, toward the renewed possibility of dialogue. "To ac-knowledge" is a way of keeping faith—a faith without religion—that there will always be something beyond the violence of predicative verbs; that there is always the possibility of a future together that defies the need for violence. Without this ac-knowledgment; without this conditioning that structures language and secures respect amidst the warring of words and predicative sentences, there would be no renewed opinions, no free-speech, no book on Derrida and Africa.

So what of these chapters? What can be learned from these chapters and the way they steadfastly secure, in their own ways, respect for Derrida and Africa? Can we talk of a conditioning of the other in these chapters? Let's survey tangentially and not exhaustively what occurs in the preceding pages. Since the chapters contained in this book are already written and are therefore, somehow, "fixed knowledge" and not a live debate, this survey necessarily takes the shape of a straightforward analysis of the textual form of respect contained herein, albeit one that could never be qualified of "deconstructive" properly speaking.

Firstly, respect comes in the shape of the obligatory quotation (Farred, Steyn, Kavwahirehi, Janz, Bragg, Drabinski). To respect Derrida is to quote him, that is, to take possession of portions of Derrida's thought and to graft (*graphein*) them in a foreign writing, even if what is quoted is utterly out of context, a total betrayal of his thinking. These obligatory quotations are invariably accompanied by mandatory contexualizations (Farred, Steyn, Kavwahirehi) in the shape of literature reviews justifying the borrowing and/or the new writing. Quoted and contextualized, these scholars thus push further Derrida's thought, maintaining it alive, extending the arch of his thought a little longer, thus reaching out to new readers. As such, the thought of Derrida continues respectfully over and beyond his grave, enjoining others to think with him in a trajectory that knows no closure, an ac-knowledgment that never reduces the other, here, now—but also, later, in a hundred years time, who knows—to the Same as them: the scholars in the preceding pages or even Derrida himself. Through such quotation and contextualization, these scholars' writings *condition* this unfathomable alterity that secretly maintains respect, thus extending the ethical imperative to continue reading and studying Derrida a little further still.

Respect also comes in these scholars' modes of address. Right from the start, Farred asks, "how to find a form that suits Derrida?" "How to find a form fitted to the work of thinking Derrida and Africa?" Respect here manifests itself in the way these scholars respond to Derrida's injunction to write, not just how to write about him or his works, but above all how to write in his name, in the continuation of his thought. This does not show a simple obedience to the injunction of adopting a Derridean style of writing in order to match thought with form; this simply exposes the difficulty of writing if not philosophy, at least in the margins of philosophy. In other words, to ask "what form to take" necessarily assumes that the form of philosophy is not yet fixed, archived, or museified; that it can still be invented, that philosophy can still surprise itself. As such, these scholars, like Derrida himself in his time, come up with new forms of address that encourage philosophy to never stylize itself once and for all, but seek to keep itself open, an ac-knowledgment of mystery still to be fathomed. And with these new forms or mysteries, these scholars ultimately *condition* again, this time formally, this unfathomable alterity that maintains philosophy not just alive, but ultimately, unrecognizable.

This inventive approach to the modes of address is obviously a common tactic in any Derridean context, but it comes to the fore in a remarkable way when the topic addressed is "Africa." Two themes seem to predominate the preceding chapters: origins and ends. The former is most blatantly encapsulated in the tentative gesture of thinking the mother (Bragg), Derrida's mother, mother Africa, and how it is impossible to think without first ac-knowledging this figure that gives birth to thought itself. The latter is predictably embodied by expressions of mourning (Farred, Janz, Bragg), this impossible mourning that is never achieved, never successful, and yet needs to take place at all cost. The juxtaposition of the two (origins and ends) marks the very Derridean tactic of focusing on liminal topologies, invaginated topographies, and on steps that are also "non-steps" as such. Once again, this strategy marks a type of respect that effectively calls for more, for pushing the boundaries or horizons of the idea of "Africa" so that "it" never settles, geographically or thematically: *becoming* the mother of (future) thought, *being* the (past) death that can never be mourned properly. This inventive approach thus slowly *conditions* this necessary radical alterity that here, most poignantly, has no start or end properly speaking.

Respect also comes in the way the scholars in this edited collection desperately try to locate Derrida somehow *in* Africa, quoting not only Algeria, but also more broadly, the Maghreb (Farred, Steyn, Kavwahirehi, Janz, Bragg, Drabinski) as if this region of north-west Africa manages on its own to excuse Derrida's white Sephardic European ancestry. If the Maghreb or Algeria is not referenced, then respect takes place by referring to Derrida's own interactions with other geographical parts of Africa (Steyn) or by the way European philosophy itself, with Derrida at its helm, appropriates the place of Africa (Kavwahirehi). In any case, the insecurity of having to locate him permeates this book: was he really French or was he African? Was he just a Eurocentric thinker or was he able to think beyond the confines of his Jew-Greek heritage (Steyn, Bragg)? Whatever the answer, the message is clear: in the same way that philosophy is not really Greek, but is *from* Africa, Derrida is inevitably also *from* Africa. This does not mean that philosophy and Derrida are Africans. This only means that both necessarily hail *from* Africa, this indefinite place of origin/end, that is, this radical alterity that secretly grounds Derrida's work and the work of those who link him with this vast continent. In a way, we are never finished locating Derrida—and philosophy generally—as hailing *from* Africa.

Except for Kavwahirehi, respect also comes in the way each contributor more or less appropriates the tools of deconstruction and more specifically Derrida's very own devices and cyphers. In their hands, arguments about Derrida and Africa become unsurprisingly "ill-fitting" (Farred), "a-punctual" (Farred), "out-of-joint" (Farred), "placeless" (Janz), "haunted" (Janz), "uncanny" (Janz), "uprooted" (Drabinski), and so on. It is as if it is impossible to take on a deconstructive approach to Derrida and Africa without automatically adopting the requisite implements and instruments that seek out the chips of metaphysical presence. This is no mere parroting of Derrida and his idiosyncratic methods, but a way of acknowledging his project, of letting his project live (*sur-vivre*) over and beyond Derrida himself, pushing the devices and cyphers further, that is, into a future untouched by memory or memorialization. As such, through these hackneyed deconstructive tools, these scholars condition the unexpected, the danger, the unknown to still unsettle all assurances of the same, all complacent discourses, all secured philosophy. Their well-honed deconstructive instruments thus maintain the discursive sphere open, inviting readers to ponder on the strategy of preventing both topics from closing in on themselves.

Inevitably, there is also another form of respect in the preceding chapters: a respect for Africa. This is a strange and unusual form of respect because Africa is here not something lived, but reflected upon. Besides the very concrete account of the use of the hashtag #RhodesMustFall (Steyn), there are very few accounts of life in Africa. Although Derrida hails *from* Africa, his scholars don't seem to be that interested in Africa's daily and mundane lived experiences. But this should not be seen as if these authors are just abstract thinkers uninterested in the banalities of the daily events of an entire continent. On the contrary, these contributors all attempt to give Africa its due, to be fair to its heterogeneity and multifaceted expressions. This is evident in the way that at no point in the previous chapters there is an attempt to define Africa, to identify it as this or that ("Sub-Saharan," for example) or to determine it thematically or theoretically once and for all. Africa remains like Derrida's thought open, "to come" (*à-venir*). Africa can never be settled (Farred). Africa can only remain to be thought (Farred). Africa can only be understood as a haunting (Janz). Africa is necessarily always already uprooted (Drabinski). Africa is necessarily an end which is also a beginning (Bragg, Kavwahirehi), and so on. As such, the respect that these scholars show to Africa is to avoid all easy reductionism and to ac-knowledge that a vast set of countries on earth, each with trillions of events taking place every second of time, is always already structured as futural. The conditioning here is as strong as it possibly can.

Finally, respect for Africa also comes in the way the above writers focus on specific aspects of Africa that Derrida himself did not address in his life time. The idea here is not to shame Derrida in not having spoken or written about African issues while he was alive (his silence on the Rwandan Genocide, for example, is a case in point), but to encourage a Derridean thinking of Africa so as to demonstrate not only that his thought and his deconstructive methods are still relevant, but that they are *necessary* to carry on making sense of Africa. Can we make sense, for example, of violence in South Africa without the openness of thought that Derrida advocates for? Can we make sense, to take another example, of the legacy of colonialism without the suggestion that any thought on this legacy is necessarily structured by a conditioning of the alterity of the other? Can we make sense of all the clichés about Africa (rhythm, orality, for example) without taking on board Derrida's necessary ac-knowledgment, this trajectory of thought that never settles, thus leaving the clichés suspended as if in midair, uncertain, questionable? If the answer is yes, then fascism, totalitarianism, chauvinism, and racism are our lot. If the answer is no, then all African issues (past, present, or future) remain somewhat unaddressed, their radical alterity staying if not secured, at least conditioned a little longer still.

And the same is true for the preceding chapters and the way they will be read. If the outcome of this future reading is: "this chapter is good," "this chapter is bad," then dogmatism, doctrinairism, and disciplinarian divisions continue to reign supreme. This edited collection of chapters on Derrida and Africa becomes foreclosed, unredeemable, already obsolete, yet another dusty book abandoned on a library shelf. If the outcome is, on the contrary, a renewed pledge to keep the reader in mystery, then everything is not lost, something manages to somehow resist the violence of judgment. The book will then on occasion elicit further reflections and additional debates on this man and this continent, their cultures and their manifold trajectories. In between the two, there will always be, *of course*, many forms of disrespect, many contemptuous "no" to both topics, many passing-byes without a glance toward this, no doubt, already dusty library book. But who really will dare to say "no" to both the man who once lived in Paris and/or this continent of over a billion people? Who will be mad enough to avoid this invitation to continue thought or to ignore the conditioning of the very radical alterity of the other? However much future readers can and will steer clear of this edited collection of chapters, respect will still somehow prevail. Thought will continue its a-destinal trajectory.

NOTES

1. Jacques Derrida, "Violence and Metaphysics: An Essay on the Thought of Emmanuel Levinas," trans. by Alan Bass, in *Writing and Difference* (London: Routledge, 2001), 182. Henceforth abbreviated as Derrida, "Violence and Metaphysics."
2. This variance occurs mainly in the section entitled "On Ontological Violence," in Derrida, "Violence and Metaphysics," 167-92.
3. Derrida, "Violence and Metaphysics," 172.

WORK CITED

Derrida, Jacques. "Violence and Metaphysics: An Essay on the Thought of Emmanuel Levinas." Translated by Alan Bass. In Writing and Difference. London: Routledge, 2001), 97–192.

Index

accusative, 20
Algeria, xi, xii, xiii, xiv, xvii, xviii, xx, xxv, xxix, 2, 4, 5, 6, 7, 9, 10, 11, 12, 13, 18, 20, 23, 35, 43, 47, 66, 75, 91
alibi, xxvii, 6, 7
alterity, 8, 20, 21, 22, 88, 89, 90, 91, 92, 93
Althusser, Louis, xv, 71
Amo, Antoine Guillaume, 67, 68, 72, 81
anarchic, 30, 50
an-archy, xviii
ancestors, 7, 8, 9, 10, 11, 13
anti-apartheid, xix, 56, 61n23
anti-colonial, 28, 70
anti-semitism, xii, xviii, xxviii
apartheid, xix, 47, 50, 51, 52, 55, 56, 59, 61n13, 61n24, 62n36, 63n37
apologia, xv, xxvii, 70
aporia, 7
Appiah, Kwame Anthony, 67, 81n13, 83
arrival, 9, 26, 39, 40, 41, 42, 43
atavistic, 24
Augustine, xx, xxiii, 47, 67, 72
autoimmunity, xxx, 19, 29

Barthes, Roland, xi, xv, xvi, xviii, xix, xxv, xxix, 9
birth, xv, xviii, xxvi, 18, 36, 37, 38, 39, 40, 41, 43, 47, 79, 90
Boulaga, Eboussi, 76, 77, 78
Butler, Judith, 36, 37

Casey, Edward, 1, 3
Celan, Paul, 26
cenotaph, 25, 26
Césaire, Aimé, 73
cinder, xvii, xxi, xxiv, 2, 8, 9, 24, 25, 26, 28, 29
citizenship, 7, 19

colonial, xxx, 17, 19, 28, 41, 52, 53, 54, 55, 59, 60, 61n24, 62n36, 63n43, 69, 71, 74
colonialism, xviii, 12, 22, 30, 34, 41, 53, 56, 60, 69, 70, 92
community, 8, 10, 29
cosmopolitanism, 20, 24
creolization, 22, 30

death, xv, xvi, xxiv, xxv, xxvii, xxviii, xxix, 7, 8, 9, 10, 19, 24, 25, 26, 27, 28, 29, 30, 39, 48, 55, 59, 90
de Certeau, Michel, 6
decolonization, 19, 35, 74
deconstruction, 3, 4, 18, 19, 22, 23, 25, 26, 27
deferral, 2, 3, 4, 7, 25
Deleuze, Gilles, xv, 4, 10, 11, 12
deterritorialization, 11, 19, 66, 81
diachronic, 20
diaspora, xi, xxii, 4, 18, 19, 23, 24, 26, 27, 28, 29, 30, 31
diasporic, xii, 18, 19, 21, 26, 27, 29, 30
différance, 18, 19, 20, 24
disfigurement, xvi
dislocation, 18
displacement, 3, 4, 19, 20, 27, 29, 30, 55, 76, 77
Dussel, Enrique, 73, 74, 75, 77
dwelling, 1, 3, 4, 5, 11, 12, 18, 19, 28, 29

El Biar, xii, xiii, xviii, xix, xx, xxiii, xxv, xxvi, xxvii, xxix, xxx
Enlightenment, 72
Ereignis, 4, 25
example, 1, 47, 48, 50, 51, 54, 56, 57, 59, 60, 61n24
exemplarity, 47, 48, 54, 57

Fanon, Frantz, 5, 34, 35, 40, 42, 50, 56, 57, 61n14, 75
femininity, 38
forgiveness, 47, 49, 51
Foucault, Michel, xiii, xv, 5, 71, 74, 80
franco-Maghrebian, xii, 19, 23, 26, 27
francophone, xi, 65, 66
freedom, xvi, xviii, xx, xxii, xxvi, xxix, 59
Freud, Sigmund, 37, 38

geography, 17, 19, 65, 66
ghostly, xxii, 7
Glissant, Édouard, xix, 22, 30
Greekjew, 18
Guattari, Félix, 11, 19, 65
Gyekey, Kwame, 10

Hamlet, xxii, xxiv, xxvii
Hani, Chris, xxiii, 50, 51
hashtag, 47, 50, 54, 57, 58, 59, 60, 62n34, 92
haunting, xii, xviii, xxi, xxv, 2, 7, 8, 9, 10, 11, 13, 43, 58, 85, 92
Hegel, G.W.F., 11, 47, 74, 75, 78, 79
Heidegger, Martin, xi, xxvii, xxviii, 1, 3, 4, 11, 12, 18, 27, 28, 29, 42, 72, 74, 79, 80, 86
hermeneutics, 33
hospitality, 2, 5, 7, 19, 21, 40, 41, 42
Hountondji, Paulin, 67, 68, 69, 71, 74, 75, 76, 79
Husserl, Edmund, 20, 23, 27
hyphen, 24, 26, 27, 28, 29, 30, 31, 60, 87, 88

identification, 10, 17, 20, 41, 66, 87
imagination, xv, 17, 18, 22, 34, 35
inheritance, xxii, xxiii, 3, 19, 38, 59
intersubjectivity, 20

Jameson, Frederic, xv, xxxin8
Jewgreek, 18
justice, xv, xxx, 11, 19, 41, 51, 59, 61n23

Kant, Immanuel, xviii, 1, 12, 75, 80
Khatibi, Abdelkebir, 74
khōra, 1, 2, 3, 6, 7, 12, 13

Latour, Bruno, 33
Liebniz, G.W., xxvii
Levinas, Emmanuel, xv, 18, 20, 21, 22, 27, 85, 86, 88, 89
logocentrism, 2, 3, 38
logos, 86

Maghreb, xviii, xx, xxiii, xxv, xxix, 18, 27, 28, 74, 91
Maghrebian, xii, xix, 2, 19, 23, 24, 26, 27, 28
Malabou, Catherine, 2, 11
Mandela, Nelson, xix, 47, 49, 51, 59, 60, 62n36, 63n37, 63n43, 63n48
Marx, Karl, xxiii, xxiv, 8
maternity, 35, 36, 37, 38, 39, 40, 41, 42, 43
Maxwele, Chumani, 52, 53, 55, 59
Mediterranean, 19, 23, 26, 30
melancholia, xvi, 55
metaphor, xv, 26, 69, 71, 74, 79
monolingualism, 5, 11, 19, 20, 21, 22, 25, 27, 28, 29, 30, 55
mother, xv, xvi, xxiv, 9, 35, 36, 37, 38, 39, 41, 43, 90
mourning, xi, xv, xvi, xx, xxvi, xxvii, xxviii, 2, 8, 9, 13, 19, 24, 25, 26, 60, 85, 90
Mudimbe, V.Y., 69, 70, 71, 72, 74, 75, 79, 80

Naas, Michael, 10, 37, 38
Nancy, Jean-Luc, xviii, xxii, xxviii, xxix
nationalism, 38
Nelson, Willie, xxvi, xxix
neocolonial, 50
Nietzsche, Friedrich, 11, 74
North Africa, 47, 67
nostalgia, xvii, 6, 24

ontotheology, 2
opacity, 22
origin, xviii, xx, 7, 11, 17, 23, 27, 29, 37, 38, 39, 40, 43, 47, 50, 51, 55, 66, 67, 68, 69, 71, 75, 81, 90

pharmakon, 19
photography, xv, xviii

place, xii, xiii, xix, xx, xxiv, xxvi, xxviii, xxix, 1, 2, 3, 4, 5, 6, 7, 8, 9, 10, 11, 12, 13, 18, 19, 21, 27, 29, 40, 41, 43, 48, 60, 65, 66, 71, 72, 73, 74, 76, 77, 78, 79, 80, 81, 85, 88, 91
poetry, xv, xvi, 80
poly-vocal, 50
postcolonial, xi, xii, xviii, xxx, 2, 5, 34, 43, 66, 71, 72, 74, 78
Presocratic, 24, 29
punctum, xix, 9

racism, 11, 53, 55, 70, 76, 92
respect, 85, 86, 87, 88, 89, 90, 91, 92, 93
responsibility, xiv, xv, xxii, xxvi, xxvii, 6, 7, 20, 42, 59
reterritorialization, 11, 19
retrieval, 18
Rhodes, Cecil John, 50, 51, 52, 53, 54, 55, 56, 57
Ricoeur, Paul, 33, 71

Said, Edward, 20
Sartre, Jean-Paul, xv, xxxin8, 34, 69, 70, 71, 75, 80
Sedgwick, Eve, 33
Senghor, Léopold, 69, 79
Shakespeare, William, xxii, xxvii, 58, 62n31
simulacrum, 22, 29
singularity, xiii, xv, 34, 36, 38, 49, 50, 54, 56, 60

Socrates, xxvi, xxviii
South Africa, xix, 6, 47, 53, 57, 58, 60, 61n24, 62n36, 63n37, 63n43, 63n48, 92
sovereignty, xxiv, 36, 37, 39, 41, 71
spatiality, 1, 19, 23
spectre, 1, 7, 12
subjectivity, 20, 21, 22, 29, 34, 35, 36, 39, 41

Tempels, Placide, 69
temporality, 19, 20, 23, 42
territorialization, 19, 38, 65, 66, 81
Timbuktu, 67
tomb, 9, 24, 25, 26, 28
trace, xvii, xx, xxi, 6, 7, 11, 28
transcendental, 19
truth, xv, xvi, xviii, xx, xxxin7, 18, 73, 76, 79, 87

Ugirashebuja, Octave, 79, 80
undecidable, 28, 30

vernacular, xv, 30, 31
violence, xiii, xv, xvii, xx, xxi, 18, 25, 27, 28, 29, 41, 50, 55, 70, 74, 86, 89, 92, 93

Williams, Raymond, 33
Williams, William Carlos, xxiv
wound, xv, xvi, 9, 12, 74

About the Editor

Grant Farred is the author, most recently, of a trilogy of works on sport and the event. These works are *Entre Nous: Between the World Cup and Me* (Duke University Press, 2019), *The Burden of Over-representation* (Temple University Press, 2018) and *In Motion, At Rest: The Event of the Athletic Body* (University of Minnesota Press, 2013). His other publications include *Martin Heidegger Saved My Life* (University of Minnesota Press, 2015) and *What's My Name? Black Vernacular Intellectuals* (University of Minnesota Press, 2003).

About the Contributors

Nicolette Bragg is a postdoctoral fellow at the University of Delaware, with a PhD in English Language and Literature from Cornell University. She works in twentieth- and twenty-first-century World Literature, Critical Theory, and Feminism and Gender Studies, with an emphasis on the theory and philosophy of maternity. She has published in *Cultural Studies Review* and *The Journal of French and Francophone Philosophy*. Her dissertation, "Creature of Theory: Maternity and the Touch of Language," explores the maternity of influential critical theory, focusing on later works of Jacques Derrida, Judith Butler, and Michel Foucault.

John Drabinski is Charles Hamilton Houston 1915 Professor in the Department of Black Studies at Amherst College. He writes and publishes on the philosophical dimensions of the black Atlantic intellectual tradition, with particular focus on the work of Édouard Glissant and James Baldwin. He is the author of four books, including most recently *Glissant and the Middle Passage: Philosophy, Beginning, Abyss* (Minnesota, 2019).

Bruce B. Janz is professor in the Department of Philosophy, codirector of the Center for Humanities and Digital Research, and Texts and Techology Ph.D. Program core faculty member, all at the University of Central Florida. He has taught in Canada, Kenya, and South Africa, as well as the United States. He researches and writes in African philosophy, contemporary European philosophy, digital humanities, and on questions of place and space across disciplines.

Kasereka Kavwahirehi is professor of French at the University of Ottawa, Canada. He is a specialist of Francophone literature with interest in postcolonial studies and African philosophy. His recent publications include: *V.Y. Mudimbe et la réinvention de l'Afrique. Poétique et politique de décolonisation des sciences humaines* (2006), *L'Afrique, entre passé et futur: l'urgence d'un choix public de l'intelligence* (2009), *Le prix de l'impasse. Christianisme africain et imaginaires politiques* (2013), and *Y en a marre. Philosophie et espoir social en Afrique* (2018).

Jean-Paul Martinon is reader in visual cultures and philosophy at Goldsmiths College, University of London. He has written monographs on a Victorian workhouse (*Swelling Grounds*, Rear Window, 1995), the idea of the future in the work of Derrida, Malabou and Nancy (*On Futurity*, Palgrave, 2007), the temporal dimension of masculinity (*The End of Man*, Punctum, 2013), and the concept of peace after the Rwandan genocide (*After "Rwanda,"* Rodopi, 2013). He is also the editor of *The Curatorial: A Philosophy of Curating* (Bloomsbury, 2014). His next book, *Curating as Ethics* will be published in 2020 by Minnesota University Press. www.jeanpaulmartinon.net.

Jan Steyn teaches French and literary translation at the University of Iowa. In addition to being a literary scholar and translation theorist, he is a practicing literary translator from Afrikaans, Dutch, and French, most recently translating Fatou Diome's *La Préference Nationale* for Archipelago Books. He holds a PhD in Comparative Literature from Cornell University and his scholarship has been published in *Translation Review* and *PoCo Pages*. You can find his recent reviews in *LARB*, *The White Review*, *Music & Literature*, and *The Quarterly Conversation*. His forthcoming projects include a chapter on "Coetzee and Translation" in the *Cambridge Companion to J.M. Coetzee*, a chapter on "Comparative Studies" in the *De Gruyter's Handbook of Anglophone World Literatures*, an edited volume to be published by Cambridge UP entitled *Translation: Crafts, Contexts, Consequences*, and a monograph about the concept of contemporaneity in world literature.

www.ingramcontent.com/pod-product-compliance
Lightning Source LLC
Chambersburg PA
CBHW050910300426
44111CB00010B/1462